Endorsements for *Gifts of Passage*

"In this compelling book, Amy Hollingsworth's remarkable gift with words unfolds a thesis that is both powerful and gentle: there are gifts left at the time of passage. The outcome is a wonderfully comforting perspective on life's final transition."

—Squire Rushnell, bestselling author of *When God Winks*

"Amy Hollingsworth has given us a wonderful gift in this book, enabling us to view death from a new and different perspective, which is a rare gift indeed. I can honestly say I have never thought about discerning the gifts that loved ones wanted to give us before their deaths, whether intentionally or unintentionally. Yet it makes perfect sense to me now, for they do want desperately to give us one last gift before they die. Hollingsworth uses stories, literature, dreams, and biblical examples to awaken in us the desire and even a sense of holy urgency to discover, understand, and cherish these gifts. It made me ponder my past losses in a new way. I received gifts I did not know were there. I cannot thank Amy enough."

—Gerald Sittser, Professor of Theology at Whitworth University and bestselling author of *A Grace Disguised: How the Soul Grows Through Loss*

"Amy Hollingsworth's writing is reminiscent of Henri Nouwen in its vulnerability."

—Sean Herriott, host of national Catholic radio program *Morning Air*™ on Relevant Radio®

"If you have lost someone in death, this profound book will give you peace—and insight! Amy Hollingsworth boldly shares her wounded heart, after the death of her father, in the writing style and poignant insight of C. S. Lewis. In the midst of grinding pain and tears, Amy gives hope, spiritual support, and optimistically encourages people to look for the gift that their loved one has left behind.

"Amy was one of my encouragers as I walked through the pain of losing my wife to breast cancer. Amy writes from real life —she has been where you are! She is authentic, vulnerable, and radiates a warm connection with God."

—JIM CONWAY, PhD, PRESIDENT OF MID-LIFE DIMENSIONS,
AN INTERNATIONAL COUNSELING AND CONFERENCE MINISTRY.
AUTHOR OF *Traits of a Lasting Marriage*, *When a Mate Wants Out*,
Men in Mid-life Crisis, AND *Women in Mid-Life Crisis*.

GIFTS

of

PASSAGE

WHAT THE DYING TELL US WITH THE GIFTS THEY LEAVE BEHIND

AMY HOLLINGSWORTH

THOMAS NELSON
Since 1798

NASHVILLE   DALLAS   MEXICO CITY   RIO DE JANEIRO   BEIJING

Published in Nashville, Tennessee, by Thomas Nelson. Thomas Nelson is a registered trademark of Thomas Nelson, Inc.

Published in association with Yates & Yates, LLP, Attorneys and Counselors, Orange, California.

Thomas Nelson, Inc. titles may be purchased in bulk for educational, business, fund-raising, or sales promotional use. For information, please e-mail SpecialMarkets@ThomasNelson.com.

Unless otherwise noted, Scripture quotations are taken from the HOLY BIBLE: NEW INTERNATIONAL VERSION®. © 1973, 1978, 1984 by International Bible Society. Used by permission of Zondervan. All rights reserved.

Scripture quotations marked KJV are from the KING JAMES VERSION.

Scripture quotations marked NLT are from the *Holy Bible*, New Living Translation. © 1996. Used by permission of Tyndale House Publishers, Inc., Wheaton, Illinois 60189. All rights reserved.

Scripture quotations marked NASB are from the NEW AMERICAN STANDARD BIBLE®. © The Lockman Foundation 1960, 1962, 1963, 1968, 1971, 1972, 1973, 1975, 1977. Used by permission.

Library of Congress Cataloging-in-Publication Data

Hollingsworth, Amy.
    Gifts of passage : what the dying tell us with the gifts they leave behind / Amy Hollingsworth.
        p. cm.
    ISBN 978-0-8499-1920-6 (hardcover)
    1. Grief—Religious aspects—Christianity. 2. Fathers—Death—Religious aspects—Christianity. 3. Hollingsworth, Amy. I. Title.
BV4905.3.H475 2008
248.8'66—dc22   2007047184

Printed in the United States of America
08 09 10 11 12 QW 9 8 7 6 5 4 3 2 1

This book is dedicated to my mother, Carmela Christin, in honor of and gratitude for many gifts, but especially for the glass-hearted necklace that still holds the love that brought me into the world.

I do love you.

CONTENTS

Gifts of Intrigue

A Gift from My Father

ACKNOWLEDGMENTS

In *Prince Caspian*, the fourth installment in C. S. Lewis's Chronicles of Narnia, the four Pevensie children have been rescued from the boarding schools of England by virtue of a magic horn, whose beckoning promptly delivers them back into Narnia. (The magic horn has replaced the wardrobe as their mode of transport, for as Aslan, the Great Lion, says, "Things never happen the same way twice.") They are traipsing through the woods with a dwarf named Trumpkin, trying to find Prince Caspian, the true heir to the Narnian throne. Lucy, the youngest Pevensie, spies Aslan off in the distance and can tell from the look on his face that he wants her to come to him. But the other Pevensie children don't see him; therefore they don't believe. A vote is taken, Lucy loses, and they continue their traipsing in the same direction. That night Lucy is awakened by Aslan's voice calling her, and this time she goes to him. She quickly explains why she didn't obey the first time—because she couldn't convince the others—and instead of commiserating with her, Aslan emits "the faintest suggestion of a growl."

He had expected her to come when he called, with or without the others. Lucy vows to go back and make things right.

"Will the others see you too?" asks Lucy.

"Certainly not at first," says Aslan. "Later on, it depends."

"But they won't believe me!" says Lucy.

"It doesn't matter," says Aslan.

In Aslan's growl was this message: Lucy knew what she had seen, knew what she had understood, and even if she couldn't convince the others, she was to heed.

Of course she had a responsibility to try to convince the others, but as Aslan pointed out, it was not so much Lucy's ability to convince as it was theirs to see. You can't make people see.

My first acknowledgment goes to Jeana Ledbetter, who saw right away, perhaps before I did. Who understood that I had to follow the call of Aslan, and the call of this book, as a matter of personal obedience, whether or not others believed. That she saw right away says infinitely more about her than about me, and her insight, encouragement, and intuitive spirituality gave me the "lion strength" necessary to write a book that sees gifts in death. A Narnian task, indeed.

To Joey Paul, who saw next, and with grace passed the baton to Greg Daniel, who with equal grace and encouragement passed it to Matt Baugher, who has been its faithful guardian ever since.

To Jennifer NcNeil, who safeguarded this book's heart. And to Greg MacLachlan, who dared to give it its face.

To Ed and Jean Bennett, for inviting me into the deepest grief of their lives and letting me stay.

To Andrea Hill, for her careful listening and understanding.

To Bernard and Bonnie Hurley, who provided a refuge from the storm, the mountain cabin that opens and closes this book, when Hurricane Ophelia blew us out of the Outer Banks.

To Bret Lott, who encouraged me first at a distance through his writing, and then up close through his correspondence. I am indebted to you for a word aptly spoken.

To Rebecca Bach of Grace Church of Fredericksburg, who stood up and recited Isaiah 50:4 when I had challenged God to be more specific.

To Kelly Moermond, my father's hospice nurse. If he was the Miracle Man, then you were the Miracle Worker.

To James and Cenia Hollingsworth, for both their visible and their invisible help.

And finally, to my strategic triad, my husband, Jeff; my son, Jonathan; and my daughter, Emily, for allowing this book to take up residence in our home and in me for the last year. A demanding visitor, it would never have ventured out on its own without your generous hospitality.

Chapter 1

OUT OF THE WOODS

I am sitting on the porch swing outside a mountain cabin, waiting for my dad to come out of the woods. Any minute I expect him to emerge from the thicket of trees that extends to my right, in his denim shirt and jeans and cowboy boots. He will probably be upset, cursing at the mess he has made trying to relieve himself in the wild. It would be payback for all the times he'd taken my sisters and me fishing as kids, only to hand us a roll of toilet paper and nod in the direction of the woods when we whined we had to go to the bathroom. Six girls, no boys, one dad. For a moment I can feel the corners of my mouth lift at the memory, then settle back into place when I look down at the small paperback in my lap, C. S. Lewis's *A Grief Observed*. I have read the book once before, years ago, when my brother-in-law's fiancée died unexpectedly. It helped me then, and I am hoping it will help me now.

How strangely stupid is grief. I have read that somewhere. It must have been written a long time ago, when *stupid* still meant to be in a stupor. To be struck senseless. Maybe initially grief does strike you senseless, but over time it does the opposite. It awakens the senses: you see, hear, feel, and smell the lost loved one everywhere. I look down at my book again, and as if to add its assent, it reads: "We now verified for ourselves what so many bereaved people have reported; the ubiquitous presence of a dead man, as if he had ceased to meet us in particular places in order to meet us everywhere."[1]

"Meet us everywhere." My eyes shift back to the woods. It is a silly expectation. Dad has never gone on vacation with my family—my husband and kids and me—before. There is no precedent for his being at that cabin. It isn't a real memory. It isn't a real expectation. Part of the reason for this trip to the mountains is to reflect on his death exactly a year ago.

There is something still to be done, between my father and me, a year after his death. As he was dying, he left me a gift. And now, as I ease out of the grief that stupefies and into the grief that awakens the senses, I am ready to discover what his gift means.

THE GIFT

I first learned that the dying give gifts from the literature the hospice nurses gave me when Dad came under their care. End-of-life giving is so characteristic of the dying that it is listed as a sign of approaching death, sandwiched between symptoms such as restlessness and congestion. It's part of the pattern, the orderly pattern of death.

This gift giving, the literature explains, is *deliberate*, and it most often occurs months before death, usually when the person discovers he has a terminal illness.

This was true of Dad. When he was first diagnosed with lung cancer, nine months before he died, he wanted me to have his Bible. He gave my son a telescope and his coveted piece of history, a souvenir from Omaha Beach in Normandy. My daughter got his animal almanac.

But these gifts were very different from Dad's final gift, bestowed in the last moments of his life, when being deliberate was no longer an option. I had never been with someone who was dying, and the intense spirituality that surrounds death surprised me. Dad seemed to be slipping into eternity by degrees, not all at once. For a time he teetered between two worlds; you could almost measure it in percentages: 80–20 one day, 90–10 the next. It was during this transition—this easing into eternity—that his gift was given.

This, of course, wasn't the mindful gift giving the hospice literature had described. I couldn't find any resource that explained these types of gifts—gifts with an otherworldly dimension because they are given during this sacred window, this brief overlap of heaven and earth.

I thought about other significant events in life, events we call rites of passage, that are also marked by gift giving. But usually the persons undergoing the passage—the baby at her baptism, the young man at his bar mitzvah, the debutante at her coming-out party—are the *recipients* of the gifts, not the *givers*. But death is different. The dying also make a passage (we even say "pass away" to describe their transition from one place to another, as if they were travelers), but they are the ones doing the giving.

That was the best way I knew to describe it; my father had given me a *gift of passage*, a gift that marked his passage.

Now I had something to call it, even if I didn't yet know what it meant.

Two Legends

My kids remind me that there is an image similar to my idea of a gift of passage in one of our favorite books, *Where the Red Fern Grows*. It is a classic boy-and-his-dog story (in this case, two dogs) that ends like *Sounder*, *Old Yeller*, and others, with the death of the boy's beloved pets.

At the end of the book, when Billy is leaving his home in the Ozarks with his family, he visits the place where his dogs are buried to say good-bye. There, at their makeshift grave site, he sees a red fern growing.

The Indians have a legend, Billy tells us, about the red fern. Its origin stems from the tragedy of two Indian children, a boy and a girl, lost in a blizzard and frozen to death. When they are found in the thaw of spring, a red fern has grown up between their forgotten bodies. The legend of the red fern holds that only an angel can plant the seeds, and the spot where the red fern grows is sacred. It is a mystic grave marker, when life springs from death. The red fern never dies.

Billy's father, a man of deep faith inclined to dismiss legends, begins to question himself: "Maybe this is God's way of helping Billy understand why his dogs died."[2]

Billy believes too: "I'm sure it is, Papa, and I do understand. I feel different now." He begins to notice things he has overlooked since his dogs died—in evidence of the grief that awakens senses.

Perhaps the red fern sets the pattern for all gifts of passage: planted by angels, they make death sacred, and they never die, because they are birthed from eternity. Even if the gift is not given during the passage, as my father's was, the seeds are planted then. Most important, they serve a divine purpose; they are God's way of helping us understand when someone dies.

I am certain I am on to something. I can't be the only one ever to have received a gift of passage. I decide to spend some time— months, a year if necessary—seeking out the gifts of others. Perhaps mining their stories will help me understand my own.

It's nice to have a guiding image, but better to have a well-lit path. The red fern had given me a powerful metaphor but no clear-cut place to start. Instead, I had to rely, as Billy had done, on noticing things I'd overlooked. It was only after many months had passed that I realized another ancient legend had guided my way—not of the red fern but of the red thread. The Chinese believe that an invisible red thread binds those who are destined to be together. Parents who adopt children—especially from foreign countries—often use the imagery to illustrate the providence of unexpected kinship. I didn't realize it at the time, but when I began my search to find the meaning of my dad's dying gift, I was taking hold of a red thread. Over the next months my red thread would wend its way, crossing time and culture, spanning age and death—connecting me to those whose stories would matter to me, would teach me. Each gift unraveled like a mystery, so that I was learning not only about the gift but about the *process* I had to go through to discern my own. With each story the red thread tightened, pulling me closer to the meaning of Dad's final gift.

Looking back, I shouldn't have been surprised by the first person the red thread bound me to. It was the man whose story of grief lay in my lap as I sat on the porch swing, waiting for Dad to come out of the woods.

GIFTS

of LOVE

Chapter 2

THE FOURTH LOVE

It is to a poet a thing of awe to find that his story is true.

—Isak Dinesen

C. S. Lewis is walking with a friend—a fellow by the name of Tolkien—and they happen upon a beggar. The man asks Jack, as C. S. Lewis is called by his friends, for a few shillings. Jack reaches deep into his pocket and empties its contents into the beggar's hands. Tolkien quickly rebukes him: "Jack, you shouldn't have given that fellow all that money; he'll just spend it on drink." Jack's reply is just as quick: "Well, if I had kept it, I would have only spent it on drink."[1]

I probably wouldn't have believed this story had I not interviewed Lewis's stepson when I worked in television. He was quick to disabuse me of Lewis's sainthood; somewhere in between my gushes of overadulation, he surmised my estimation of his stepfather was perhaps a little naive. But still I harbored a secret belief that when it came to spiritual matters, I could count on Lewis with a blessed assurance.

That's why I had taken his little paperback with me to the mountains. *A Grief Observed* is a chronicle of Lewis's own grief after the death of his wife, journal notes he scratched out in the blank spaces of partially used notebooks he found around the house. Certainly his experience could shed light on the meaning of Dad's dying gift. Even though I had read the book before, my need was greater now, my senses more ready to receive. But a few pages in, I quickly discovered that my genius of consolation had crumbled under the weight of the task. "Life is messy," says Garrison Keillor, "and if you experience it close up and not just from books, you're going to be inconsistent."[2] And C. S. Lewis was being inconsistent.

The man who had nurtured my own fledgling faith with his defense of the gospel was now writing in a new way about his ever-present help in times of trouble: "Go to [God] when your need is desperate, when all other help is vain, and what do you find? A door slammed in your face, and a sound of bolting and double bolting on the inside. After that, silence."[3]

As his anger intensified with each page, I held the book at arm's length to avoid the thunderstroke meant for him.

THE FOURTH LOVE

An Oxford don equally acclaimed for his nonfiction apologetics (*Mere Christianity*) and his fictional fantasies (the Chronicles of Narnia), Clive Staples Lewis was an old bachelor whose life was meticulously organized into what a close friend called "neat certainties."

One of these "neat certainties" was the way he quartered love, dividing it into four tidy categories: affection, friendship, the love of God, and erotic love. He wrote convincingly on the subject in his highly regarded *The Four Loves*, but the truth is that while Lewis had known and experienced affection, friendship, and the love of God, he had lived more than half a century without ever knowing the fourth, what he called "that kind of love which lovers are 'in.'"[4] Things were about to change for the inveterate bachelor, though, in an unexpected and sometimes eyebrow-raising turn of events.

The reality behind Lewis's love affair is a problem of "it depends on who you ask," but in essence it is this: Joy Davidman Gresham, a New York writer, poet, and former Communist, was living in the United States with her husband, novelist Bill Gresham, when she first mailed a letter to the esteemed C. S. Lewis from across the pond. Joy, an atheistic Jew, had become a recent convert to Christianity and found Lewis's apologetical works especially helpful in understanding her newfound faith. Boy meets girl, and they become pen pals. Joy's mental agility and wit made her Lewis's intellectual equal, and as their correspondence continued, the seesaw of one-sided admiration began to level out.

Joy met Jack (for she was now part of the inner circle that knew him as Jack) for the first time when she visited England with her two young sons, a couple of years after her first letter arrived. Her marriage to Bill Gresham was dissolving, and she made the trip to England in part to escape what her son told me was his father's drinking problem, although others attribute Joy's departure to Bill's inconstancy. There the relationship between Joy and Jack progressed from a mutual respect to friendship. Joy and her sons returned to the United States when she learned that Bill had set up house with another woman. Since Bill was immovable, Joy agreed to divorce and was awarded custody of their sons. She returned to England for a fresh start.

Things went well for two years, until Joy tried to renew her residence permit and was turned down without explanation. Jack, now a close friend, married Joy in the Oxford registry office in order to save her and the boys from deportation. A marriage of convenience, a mere formality, most were told, and with that, the nearly sixty-year-old professor sloughed off his bachelorhood.

The two lived apart until Joy was diagnosed with cancer the following year and did not want to die in the hospital. Jack didn't feel he could bring her into his home unless they were married in the eyes of God, so their civil union was solemnized in a religious ceremony performed at the hospital.

Whether they experienced "that kind of love which lovers are 'in'" following their proper wedding or whether it had been there all along is also a debated question. But what is not in question is that they were now very much in love, and when Joy's death sentence was commuted by the cancer's remission, they enjoyed three and a half blissful years together as husband and wife. "They learned from each other the mysteries of [love] at a depth that makes them kin to the great lovers found in literature," said the same friend who chided Lewis for his neat certainties.[5]

But the miraculous reversal was only a reprieve, and when Joy's cancer returned, it stayed for good.

Jack had loved and lost, unwilling to concede to Tennyson that it was indeed better.

BEAUTY AND THE BEAST

I left the mountain cabin at the end of my week of reflection, having reread Lewis's chronicle of grief, thinking I understood the gift that Joy had left her beloved Jack in passage. The answer could be found, I was sure, in the last five words she spoke to him before she died, which he dutifully recorded in his journal. I was proud of myself for being such a good student of my new teacher, for having arrived at my own neat certainties. But my self-congratulation was premature. Perhaps that was my first and most needful lesson: gifts of passage aren't always self-evident. Sometimes you have to sit and wait on them; there's no way to know where the seeds are planted until the red fern begins to push its way out of the soil.

For days the thought nagged at me that the answer was not found solely in Lewis's journal accounts, where most people are most honest. His autobiographical writings had in the past been less than forthright. One friend said that his memoir *Surprised by Joy* should have been titled *Suppressed by Jack*, given what was *not* in it. It became apparent to me that the key to Joy's gift, the key to understanding the impact of Joy's gift, would be found in a work of Lewis's fiction, where the master of ivory-tower reserve opened himself up most vulnerably.

I'd like to say I did my homework and pinpointed the book by careful study and process of elimination. But it wasn't a practical or even a conscious decision. Instead, I relied on something else, a kind of spiritual intuition—like Billy's noticing things—that I didn't have before I experienced the deepest grief of my life. The intuition springs, I think, from suddenly belonging to a community of mourners through which you share—if nothing else—this common ground of having loved and lost. Grief is the passkey, the secret handshake that admits you into the experiences and wisdom of this community of grievers, past and present. Somehow this shared sense gave me the push in the right direction.

It led me straight to Lewis's most dismal failure of a book, his one big flop—a souped-up version of *Beauty and the Beast* in which the beast is not a handsome prince under a spell but an ugly stepsister under a veil.[6] Hollywood may have been enamored of Lewis's relationship with Joy enough to make it into a major motion picture (*Shadowlands*) and of his fiction to make the Chronicles of Narnia into special-effects extravaganzas, but Tinseltown would never come calling for this one.

The book was Lewis's *Till We Have Faces*, a retelling of the myth of Psyche and Cupid, a love story that haunted Lewis for most of his life. He had attempted to retell the story of the union of soul (Psyche) and love (Cupid) through poetry as a teen and through a play in his twenties. His love for Joy must have been the catalyst that shook it free, and it was published with a dedication to her, a gesture that would have been more romantic had the story not been told from the vantage point of the ugly stepsister.

But in truth, comparisons have been made between this main character and Joy (who was not nearly as attractive as Debra Winger, her cinematic counterpart). The greater similarity, though, lies in personality, as, despite her appearance, the ugly stepsister is the strongest and most intricately developed female character Lewis ever created. She is capable of fierce loyalty and fiercer love.

The gist of the myth is this: Psyche is the Beauty condemned to die but rescued at the last minute by Cupid, the god of love. She is whisked away to a palace only she and her love-god can see. To continue in eternal bliss, she is forbidden to look upon her husband, who comes to her under cloak of night. The ugly stepsister—the Beast to her Beauty—urges her to do so anyway.

Psyche is then banished from the castle and wanders the world in search of redemption.

In the original myth, the sister ruins Psyche because she is jealous of the castle. In Lewis's version, the sister is not nearly as petty; she has loved and cared for Psyche as if she were her daughter. Her jealousy has nothing to do with castle envy but with having to share the object of her love: "What should I care," she rails, "for some horrible, new happiness which I hadn't given her and which separated her from me?"[7]

Lewis echoes this same sentiment after Joy's death: "They tell me [Joy] is happy now, they tell me she is at peace. What makes them so sure of this? . . . How do they know she is 'at rest'? Why should the separation (if nothing else) which so agonizes the lover who is left behind be painless to the lover who departs?"[8]

So perhaps the ugly stepsister is less Joy and more Jack. Lewis is unconsciously foreshadowing his own pain, prefiguring himself as the one bereft of love when a "new happiness" separates him from Joy, who now resides with the god of love.

Lewis becomes the beast in his own love story. And like his creation, his only recourse is to cry out in pain and rail against the One who rescued Joy from death, even if there is a twice-bolted door between them.

Eye on the Sparrow

When author Joan Didion unexpectedly lost her husband, fellow writer John Gregory Dunne, to a heart attack, she, too, picked up Lewis's little paperback and held it in her lap, waiting. Still, she was surprised that while "grief remained the most general of afflictions, its literature seemed remarkably spare," and decided to make her own contribution.[9] The result was her best-selling, award-winning *The Year of Magical Thinking*, which has since been made into a Broadway play and nominated for a Tony. She has become the modern-day voice of grief, and she relates her experience with the same honesty as Lewis, and over the same loss, a spouse.

I was not a reader of Joan Didion before my father died, although he was. I remember seeing a copy of her collection of essays, *Slouching Towards Bethlehem*, in the doll case he converted into a bookshelf for our family room. The memoir of her grief (redoubled by the subsequent death of her daughter, her only child, who lay in a coma when her husband died) has been read by millions because it is deeply moving and painfully descriptive of what grief feels like. She was, like Lewis, stupefied by it.

But she does not rail against God as he does. Lewis didn't stop at painting God as the Great Door Slammer; he goes on to make a case for him as "the Cosmic Sadist." Finally, he calls God—and this is when I held the book at arm's length—"the Eternal Vivisector." *Vivisection*, a term I'd only heard from animal-rights proponents, is an operation conducted on living animals for experimental purposes.

This is much different from the God of whom Jesus says, "Are not two sparrows sold for a penny? Yet not one of them will fall to the ground apart from the will of your Father" (Matt. 10:29), which then inspired the songwriter to write, "His eye is on the sparrow, and I know He watches me."

Choices are made in how we grieve, and Joan Didion chooses too. Anger toward God, although a common response to death, is conspicuously missing from her chronicle of grief; it might have served her better if it had found a place there.

I am left unsettled after I read her book, but I'm not sure why. Then one afternoon, sitting in the Ash Wednesday service, listening to the words ("For dust you are and to dust you will return"), I realize where the problem lies, why her book is able to depict my pain but not soothe it. Her words expose the truth of Ash Wednesday without engendering the hope of Easter.

Without hope, she has only one choice, one that is crueler still than anger. She chooses indifference. "No eye is on the sparrow," she wrote, and the last sad words of her book fall silently to the ground.

Red Thread of a Dream

I had a dream about C. S. Lewis during this time of discerning his gift from Joy. The red thread must weave its way through dreams, too, as a way of drawing people closer. In the dream I am in college, and my English professor (fittingly) has just finished his lecture. I exit the classroom and am scurrying down the stairwell of Greenlaw Hall when something slows me down, pulls at my heel. I turn around and see that my heel is caught on an article of clothing left on the stairs. But it's not just one piece; it is tied to others that I have been dragging behind me like a kite tail.

At some point I recognize the articles are "spoils of war," my term for gifts given in a dating relationship that the recipient gets to keep if the giver initiates the breakup (an unwritten code in undergraduate romance). I recognize the spoils of war because I have given them. I look up, and the culprits—a few disaffected young men—are standing there in the stairwell, facing me. (In reality, I had never given these particular gifts or broken these particular hearts, but dreams often do not bother with details.) It takes me a minute to realize I have been set up. It's a joke or a judgment from a jury of my jilted peers. I disengage the evidence from my heel and leave angrily. In the parking lot outside the classroom building, I find a friend with whom to share my story of woe. As I'm explaining the injustice, I see an old English car parked in the distance. C. S. Lewis leans his head out of the window and waves to me. I wave back, and in that instant I realize he is in on the joke.

"Natural affection, if left to mere nature, easily becomes a special kind of hatred," Lewis wrote in a letter to a friend.[10] That's what he was saying to me as well, with a wave of his hand.

He is giving me a clue in this red thread of a dream.

A special kind of hatred is what the ugly stepsister begins to feel for the sister who abandoned her, but even more so for the god who caused their separation. The object of her natural affection, the object of her fiercer love, has turned away from her to a supernatural love.

Joy's Gift

When I first heard the last words Joy spoke to Jack, I felt sure they were her gift of passage to him. Just five words before she died: "You have made me happy." Surely her gift was the assurance that the old bachelor now possessed the whole of love he had carefully divvied up. His knowledge of love was entire, consummated through their union. He had received it and, more important, given it. And there was proof: "You have made me happy."

But then I dug deeper and discovered Joy's final words were only the beginning, only part of the gift. Not a spoil of war, not a consolation prize for his broken heart, they set in motion an anguish through which the real gift was given, a gift mysteriously tied to Lewis's own creation.

At the end of his telling tale, the ugly stepsister is brought to stand trial before the god of love, against whom she has leveled her charges. She is not punished—not even humiliated, as I was in my dream—but transformed into a beauty indistinguishable from her sister.

The beauty is not the real gift; the real gift is that she learns to love, to really love, the god who separated her from her beloved.

That was Joy's real gift. Her death exposed the beast in Jack so the God of love could transform him into something beautiful. The fourth love—the one that had eluded him for most of his life—had not been romantic love after all, but a true understanding of the love of God.

"I have gradually been coming to feel that the door is no longer shut and bolted," Lewis wrote in the concluding pages of his journal, seeing the eye on the sparrow. "Was it my own frantic need that slammed it in my face? The time when there is nothing at all in your soul except a cry for help may be just the time when God can't give it; you are like the drowning man who can't be helped because he clutches and grabs. Perhaps your own reiterated cries deafen you to the voice you hope to hear."[11]

From a grief that stupefies to a grief that awakens the senses.

Lewis ends his tirade against God, in the little paperback I held in my lap, with the revelation that in her last moment of life, Joy smiled—but not at him. He follows this revelation and ends his journal for good with a few Latin words he has borrowed from Dante. Translated, they read: "And then she turned back to the Eternal."

Joy's gift, it turns out, had allowed him to do the same.

Chapter 3

HEAVEN'S PURSE

And the purses of heaven have no holes in them.

—JESUS IN LUKE 12:33 NLT

I'M SITTING ACROSS the table from Gina in a crowded book-and-coffee shop on a sunless April afternoon. Her words are retro-spect and measured, her face sad and beautiful. She is telling me about John, her fiancé, who died unexpectedly several months ago. He was her second chance at love after a difficult first mar-riage and years of going it alone. It is a love story, but its ending couldn't be more different from Joy's last moments with Jack. I have already learned that gifts of passage are not always self-evident; Gina is teaching me that they're not always wrapped up in neat little packages.

I begin to wonder what happens when life doesn't end kindly, when loved ones don't depart with a smile and healing last words. Is there still an angel present to sow the seeds of the red fern?

Does heaven offer its own gifts when the dying aren't able to? I push these questions aside for the moment to listen to Gina's story from the beginning.

Gina works with kindergartners. So if you want to win her heart, you should appeal to the childlike spirit that abides there. That's what John did when he bought her a copy of *Mattie and Cataragus* and read it to her over the phone. *Mattie and Cataragus* is a picture-book love story about a shy, quiet gentleman cat who becomes infatuated with a feline named Mattie. The relationship gets off to a shaky start, due to Cataragus's ill-fated attempts to win Mattie's attention. But this is a storybook, and by its end love prevails. Fifty-year-old John wasn't in the privacy of his home or a soundproof phone booth when he read the preschool book to Gina; he was in the crowded, noisy auto-repair shop he owned. Strapping John in a strapping place reading about two cats that fall in love.

Since Gina and John had both been married before, they weren't naive about middle-aged romance. Second chances are often long shots. They were cautious. But the day John read the amorous tale of two cats over the phone, Gina knew it was worth the risk. No bumbling attempts at love here. The two were engaged a short time later.

Still, there were problems. John worked too hard. Sometimes his dinnertime fell in with the eleven o'clock news. More than that, though, Gina noticed that he felt responsible, overly responsible, for everyone else's woes. Often customers were allowed to take home their repaired cars without paying. "How can they pay me if they can't drive to work?" John would reason. His customers became his friends, and he lent enough money to bring a mortgage account up to date for one of them. "He has kids; what else could I do?" was John's explanation that time. But in truth his own woes were sufficient. He had lost his daughter in an auto accident just days after her high school graduation. He was at the shop at the time, and his daughter was supposed to call him at noon. Nothing ever kept her from calling when she was supposed to. When noon came and went, John calmly dismissed his workers for the day and closed himself in the office, waiting for the call.

Among the things the incomprehensible loss of a child etched in John's psyche was the desire to end with loving words. He always told Gina he loved her before hanging up the phone. Once, when he was at work and ended a call abruptly, he forgot to say "I love you." Gina's phone rang again within seconds, and when she picked up, John repented of his omission. He was sorry; he had been distracted by a business concern. "We always ended with loving words," Gina said.

One Sunday afternoon, Gina volunteered to go with John on some work errands. She told a customer's wife that day, "He's going to kill himself if he keeps going like this." I asked Gina about John's medical history. He had high blood pressure, but medication leveled it out. There was no diagnosis of heart disease. During his last doctor's appointment, the doctor had said his heart was strong. John returned every three months for blood pressure checks. That was the extent of it. Friends suspected that Gina's soothing presence worked on John as effectively as any medicine the doctor could prescribe for him.

This week, though, had been stressful. John and Gina had recently returned from the funeral of one of John's favorite nieces, who had succumbed to cancer. The new loss brought renewed grief to the old one. His daughter was surely on his mind this Sunday afternoon, as the anniversary of her death was the next day. John worked even harder when he was troubled, and he was very troubled. Even on Sunday, he was still working, still handling shop business. He was more agitated than usual.

At one point in the afternoon, Gina remembers, he was so frustrated that he got in his car and drove off without telling anyone where he was going. It was out of character for John; he had never done that before. It frightened her.

When he returned home, he explained to Gina that the problem was "shop stuff." He wasn't angry at her. After watching TV for a few minutes, he got up, holding his side and complaining that his arms felt strange. It was hard to get his breath. Gina went for the phone to call the rescue squad.

John said no.

When later he complained of chest pain, Gina insisted they call 911.

Again, John said no.

An observer of this scene might wonder why Gina didn't just call 911 and override John's protests. The thing that kept Gina from calling was fear, fear that John, now more agitated than she had ever seen him, would get back in his car and drive off again. What if something happened to him while he was driving? At least this way she could be with him and make sure he was okay.

John lay down and tried to relax. He was calmer, but the chest pains continued. Gina followed him around with a big family medicine book, telling him that if lying down didn't take away the chest pains, the situation would be considered an emergency. She was going to call the rescue squad.

John had had it. "I just need to be left alone! Why can't anyone just do what I ask them to do? I don't know why my life . . ." and his voice trailed off as he left the room.

Both retreated to separate corners to cool off: John went to the front porch to sit on the glider, Gina to the back porch. There Gina rehearsed the speech she was going to give John when they made up. He needed to cut back on work hours. He needed to slow down. He needed to take the weight of the world off his shoulders. He needed to . . .

Gina got up from the back porch to go to John. He must have had the same idea, because he had left the porch and was on his way to meet her. Gina found him at the midpoint, lying motionless on the ground.

John had been distracted by a business concern and had forgotten to end with loving words.

Heaven's Song

Not all gifts of love pass between lovers (or fail to pass between lovers). There are other kinds of relationships, other times when heaven may find the need to intervene.

When Barbara Walters hosted a two-hour prime-time special about heaven, she neglected to mention its theme song. I wasn't waiting to hear a hymnbook standard such as "In the Sweet By and By" or "When the Roll Is Called Up Yonder," but a song that reached the apex of the top forty adult contemporary, gospel, and country music charts. A song that imagines what heaven will be like.

Surrounded by Your glory, what will my heart feel?

Because of its vividly moving lyrics and melody, "I Can Only Imagine" by MercyMe became an across-genres success, producing a double-platinum debut album that sold two million copies in three years. It also became a song frequently played and performed at memorial services and funerals, including my father's.

But it was the death of another father that inspired the poignant song.

I know this story because it found me at the mountain cabin at the same time C. S. Lewis's story did. I had been on the porch reading *A Grief Observed* before I walked inside to find my son watching a DVD about the making of the song. I sat down to join him. I was just beginning to conceive the idea of a gift of passage as a way to identify my father's gift when another one was presented to me to show me something important. Something that would later help to answer the questions Gina's story was asking.

Singer and songwriter Bart Millard was three when his parents divorced. As in most divorces, his mother became the custodial parent, but eventually he and his brother moved in with their father and stayed for good. Since Bart was in third grade at the time, he and his father were able to forge an especially close relationship. Bart was only eighteen when his father died of cancer in 1991.

His father's dying gift was tangible and purposed, carefully separated into dollars and cents. Bart's father had set aside money to care for him and his brother for the next ten years, in the form of a monthly check, scraped together from his $26,000-a-year salary.

But even after the ten years were up, his father assured him, "I will still be there to take care of you, somehow."[1]

Bart remembers this meeting, working out the practicalities of his father's finances at a time of such grief, as the hardest thing he'd ever done. Heaven's purse could keep the money; he just wanted his dad to live.

Growing up in the church, Bart had always heard people refer to heaven as "a better place," and he heard it more than he cared to after his father's death. If your father were given the choice now, people would say, he would choose to stay where he is. Bart accepted this on a theological level (as most people do until they lose someone they love), but on an emotional level it seemed selfish of his father. How could he choose heaven when his sons needed him? And what is it about heaven that is so irresistible it could make a father's choice so easy? Over the course of the next several years, Bart's unanswered questions twined themselves around his grief and irrupted into the private thoughts recorded in his journal.

Eight years after his father's death, Bart and his MercyMe bandmates were working on an independent record in need of a final song. Bart looked through his journal for inspiration and was surprised to find on literally every page the scribbled words, "I can only imagine." *Maybe I should finish this,* he thought. What will heaven be like? What would his heart feel?

Will I dance for You, Jesus, or in awe of You be still?

He wrote the lyrics in a matter of minutes, and "I Can Only Imagine" was recorded as a B-side song in an old Sunday school building. For months MercyMe didn't even perform it. The song was an add-on that didn't go with the rest of the record. But soon the band was getting repeated requests to play the ballad. The song began to climb the contemporary Christian music charts.

Bart's attention was diverted from the continuing success of the song when his son was born in early 2001. In a radio interview during that time, the disc jockey announced that "I Can Only Imagine" had hit number one that day. First surprised, Bart became overwhelmed by a different kind of emotion when he realized it was also the day—the very day—the last check arrived from his father.

"I will still be there to take care of you, somehow."

His father had kept his promise to take care of Bart for the ten years his meager trust had allowed. When the funds ran dry, heaven opened its purse and dropped the gift the dying person wasn't able to give, by inspiring a song that was.

HEAVEN'S FIRE

I marvel at the providence of dying gifts. Bart's father made a promise that only heaven could keep. No grieving person is left empty-handed.

But gifts are not always self-evident, nor are they always delivered in neat little packages. Sometimes they are hidden from plain sight until they are needed.

This is true in the case of Blaise Pascal, the esteemed French mathematician and philosopher, whose death three hundred years ago precludes our meeting for coffee. But the red thread doesn't care, isn't hindered by time, and stretches back through it at will to bind me to this unlikely teacher.

"The heart has its reasons of which reason knows nothing" doesn't sound like something a physicist would say,[2] but these words belong to Pascal, who, in addition to this famous quote, has a law and a wager attached to him.

Pascal's law is a reflection of his scientific side, a law of physics that has to do with fluid pressures. Pascal's wager is a reflection of his philosophical side and has to do with religion. In it he posits that belief in God is a better choice than nonbelief in God, given the eternal and irreversible consequences of nonbelief. (For example, if you do believe in God, and there is no afterlife, you've lost nothing. If you don't believe in God, and there is an afterlife, you've lost everything.) Believing in God, then, according to Pascal's reasoning, is a better "wager." The idea of Pascal, ever the mathematician, applying game theory to the Creator of the universe has led some to invent yet another term, Pascal's flaw. That Pascal would even attempt to write about religion might have left many of his seventeenth-century contemporaries slack-jawed, as they considered him a morally deficient freethinker and thought that if by some chance he were admitted into heaven, it would be due only to a last-minute pass by deathbed confession.

But Pascal had something they didn't know about. In addition to a law and a wager (and a flaw), he also had an amulet.

Pascal's amulet wasn't a magic charm that protected him against evil or a lucky charm to bring him good fortune. It wasn't even a necklace, although he wore it close to his chest. Instead, it was an old, faded scrap of paper with strange words scratched on it.

Not a living soul knew about Pascal's parchment (or the experience written on it) during his lifetime. If not for a keen-eyed servant, no one would ever have known.

After Pascal's death from lifelong ill health, just after his thirty-ninth birthday, a servant found a piece of parchment sewn into his coat jacket, where it had resided for eight years. On it was written a memorial to his "night of fire." It read, in part:

In the year of Grace, 1654,
On Monday, 23rd of November . . .
From about half past ten in the evening until about half past
Twelve,
FIRE
God of Abraham, God of Isaac, God of Jacob,
not of the philosophers and scholars.
Certitude. Certitude. Feeling. Joy. Peace.
God of Jesus Christ . . .
Joy, joy, joy, tears of joy.
I have separated myself from Him . . .
Let me not be separated from Him eternally.
"This is eternal life,
that they might know Thee, the only true God,
and Jesus Christ, whom Thou hast sent"
Jesus Christ . . .
Renunciation, total and sweet.
Total submission . . .
Eternally in joy for a day's training on earth . . . Amen.[3]

Spontaneously and inexplicably, the mathematic genius experiences two hours of rapture in which it is revealed to him that the God of Abraham, Isaac, and Jacob is not the god of the philosophers and scholars. Overcome, he who is considered one of France's most eloquent writers could only stutter out staccato responses—sentence fragments and inadequate adjectives—to describe what was happening to him.

After this experience, Pascal's "night of fire," meticulously recorded on a piece of parchment, stayed close to his heart, sewn into his jacket for the rest of his life. The man who famously wrote, "The heart has its reasons of which reason knows nothing," was writing from experience, this experience.

Pascal never told anyone about his mysterious night; it could have remained his secret. Instead, it was uncovered by an unsuspecting servant. Was it meant to be a gift, inadvertently left for the comfort of a loved one?

Or did heaven's purse have its own bet to settle? In exposing Pascal's night of fire, a gift of love of another kind, it was also setting the record straight: it was God who had made his wager for Pascal.

Heaven's Gift

Jesus said, "The purses of heaven have no holes in them" (Luke 12:33 NLT). And, of course, what he meant was that treasures stored in heaven can never be destroyed. I wonder, though, if at times God allows holes to let gifts fall through. What a songwriter and a scientist have taught me is that dying gifts are not always given at the point of passage; there are times when the death is unexpected or the gift comes later, after the death.

That's when heaven's purse has holes. But you have to know to look for them; these gifts, not wrapped up in neat little packages, may be overlooked. Pascal's servant could have thrown out the jacket without ever seeing its hidden memorial. Bart Millard could have missed the message hidden in his journal entries.

And Gina.

Two weeks after John died of a massive heart attack on his way to reconcile with her, Gina was in the attic going through some of her things, unsure what to do with the dress. It was a vestige of their life together, and she knew she couldn't wear it now.

Guilt plagued her. John's last words, his last jarring accusation—"Why can't anyone just do what I ask them to do?"—didn't apply to her. She had honored his request not to call 911. Gina later learned that agitation and anger are common symptoms of heart attacks. In a tragic way it was John's own symptoms that prevented what may have been the cure.

But still Gina couldn't quash the nagging feeling that she could have prevented it. It became an obsessive thought that she knew was a part of the grieving process. Another obsessive thought had to do with the dress.

She and John had bought it together, two months before, while shopping downtown. It was a beautiful vintage dress, but she hadn't worn it yet as the collar had been damaged. She'd put it in the attic until she could take it to a seamstress. *I can't imagine I'll ever wear it now*, she thought. *I wouldn't want to wear it for anyone else.* She had decided to give it to a local dinner theatre troupe and didn't intend to even take it out of the bag. Alone in the attic, she sensed what she called a "silent shout" that beseeched her not to give away the dress until she checked the bag. Frustrated by her self-vexing, Gina said out loud, "Fine, I will look in the bag." She took the jacket out and put it on again. That's when she saw a plastic bag and white tissue paper. No neat little package; it looked like it could have been trash.

Gina unfolded the white tissue paper to expose a beautiful silver locket, an amulet of her own.

John must have purchased it while she was looking around the vintage shop. He must have slipped it in with her dress and forgotten to give it to her. (Gina remembers he took a rare nap upon returning home that day.) Perhaps he had intended to give it to her on the day she would wear the dress for the first time. That day would never come; Gina was giving the dress away.

In deciding to do so, she had almost overlooked John's dying gift. He didn't know he was dying, but heaven did. It opened its purse and let fall a locket. Gina got her gift.

And John got his second chance to end with loving words.

GIFTS *of* PRESENCE

Chapter 4

THE GOLD RING

How should we be able to forget those ancient myths about
dragons that at the last moment turn into princesses; perhaps all
the dragons of our lives are princesses who are only waiting to see
us once beautiful and brave. Perhaps everything terrible is in its
deepest being something helpless that wants help from us.

—RAINER MARIA RILKE,
Letters to a Young Poet

TRYING TO IMAGINE what heaven might be like is more difficult for me than trying to imagine what it might *feel* like.

Not in the sense that a comfortable bed "feels like heaven" to a weary traveler or how the sun feels on your face the first day of spring weather, but what it must feel like once you're there, in heaven. Of course there is no way to know for sure, but the one time I came closest to a foretaste, I was sitting in a darkened theater, Orchestra Section 11, Row O, Seat 3. The night was filled with murder, unrequited love, and a chandelier shattering into a million pieces.

That's where I felt heaven.

Three weeks later I was back, this time with my son as my date instead of my husband, to see *The Phantom of the Opera* a second time. (It was my then seven-year-old son who got me interested in the Phantom in the first place, after watching an episode of *Wishbone* on PBS, which featured the Opera ghost's tale.) What drew me back wasn't just the debt I owed my son, or even the story—although fascinating—of improbable love between a beauty and another beast, of a dragon that at the last moment turns into a princess. Instead, it was this moment of suspension: The Phantom has climbed atop the stage, and he is up to no good, about to send the chandelier careering down upon the stage, having already deftly ridded his true love of her musical competition. He is looking straight at me as he sings—this time I'm on the seat's edge in the first row of the balcony, and we are eye to eye—issuing me a dire warning: "You will curse the day you did not do," he sings, "all that the Phantom asked of you!" Even so, I don't feel the menace, only the power of the music, the power of the spectacle: the gilded stage, the flowing costumes, the deep emotions that arise when love feels like betrayal. At that moment I am pulled in, fully surrounded, and then snatched up. It's no wonder the word *rapture* includes the sense of transport. I was moved in the literal sense, and for at least the moment (although a moment is in time, and this feels outside of it), everything else seemed insignificant.

Rarely am I so fully engaged that my internal dialogue is drowned out, muffling reminders of all the other things I should be doing at that particular moment. Instead, the Phantom's voice booms, and the music crowds out any rival thought; in quite another way he has dispatched the competition. There is something transcendent—another transport word—in the experience. A moment of tension, a pregnant stillness, and then the chandelier comes crashing down.

That's what I imagine heaven to feel like, without the jangled emotions and broken glass. A perpetual state of what was, at the time, only momentary for me. Few things this side of eternity have that ability, the power to grip and not let go. To hold perfectly still. "Nothing in all creation is so like God as stillness," Meister Eckhart once wrote.[1] Arrested, surrounded, consumed, suspended: heaven will have my full attention.

It was unexpected illumination from a masked man wreaking havoc in a Paris opera house. Thinking back on that day, I began to wonder: *If the Phantom could provide such deep insight into heaven, could he also provide insight into dying? Could he hold a clue to Dad's dying gift?* I could feel the tug of the red thread, but there was a problem. Dad's gift was real, and the Phantom wasn't.

A Historian's Duty

"The Opera ghost was real. He was not, as many thought, a figment of the imagination of all who worked at the Opera. He was a real person, but he did assume the form of a phantom, a ghost."[2] Thus begins Gaston Leroux's famous novel, published in 1910. Right away the reader is struck by the contradiction of opening a novel—a made-up story—with the declaration that the title character is indeed real. Leroux goes as far as to say his recounting of events that transpired in turn-of-the-century Paris was his "duty as a historian."

These declarations could, of course, be literary devices, but there are many who believe otherwise. Those who have invested their resources into finding out the truth behind Leroux's claim to an "incredible and yet veracious story" have uncovered striking similarities between it and elements of real life in nineteenth-century Paris.

Of course, no one doubts the existence of the setting, the Paris Opera House; with its seventeen stories, myriad trapdoors, and mysterious Box Five, it provided the ideal stage for the Phantom's intrigues. But the underground lake, upon which the Phantom transports opera ingénue Christine Daaé to his lair, was also real, a remnant of the excavation of the site in 1861. For the seven months of digging required for the foundation of the grand opera house, pumps were used around the clock to free the site of water. Still, once the foundation was laid, a large underground lake remained in the deepest cellar.

If the stage is real, what about its players? Prominent characters also have real-life counterparts: Christine's musical rival, the croaking Carlotta, is based on Mademoiselle Carvalho. Christine herself, both her character and her backstory, is based on the singer Christine Nilsson. The family of Raoul de Chagny, Christine's true love, shares the name and attributes of a French family that lived during the time Leroux was writing his novel.

And the famous shattering chandelier? Also a real event, with one death in the audience, just as Leroux reported it.

As for the Phantom himself, the mysterious man with the disfigured face hidden beneath a mask, a former Opera worker claims a skeleton with a ring on its finger was found underground early in the twentieth century, along with a house built in the cellars.

Perhaps the most compelling evidence comes from a member of Leroux's own family, his great-granddaughter Veronique. An author of a nonfiction work on the Phantom visited the Paris Opera House, meeting both Leroux's biographer and his great-granddaughter. From Veronique, the author learned that the Phantom's character—named Erik in the novel—is based on a real person who lived in the cellars. But, she conceded, her great-grandfather also "freely embellished around the facts to make a more coherent, romantic and artistic story."[3] How true was the story? Veronique figures around 70 percent.

And so when Leroux begins with "The Opera ghost was real," he means the vast majority of him was.

THE TRAPDOOR LOVER

My English professors were surprised years ago when I bounded into the registrar's office to declare a double major, adding psychology to my degree program. They shouldn't have been, though; in my mind both majors served the same purpose. In one program, you unfold and decode characters and their authors. In the other, you unfold and decode behavior and its authors. The main difference is that the subjects are fictional in the one, real in the other. Some, like the Phantom, are straddlers, and to learn from him, I would need to draw from both sides of the fence.

After seeing the musical a second time, a friend invited me over to meet an acquaintance of hers. Still brimming from my experience, I asked if the acquaintance had seen the musical. She had. She didn't like it. When I asked her why, she reluctantly offered, "I thought the Phantom was, well, mean."

What came out of my mouth then, as a twice-degreed unfolder and decoder, was only a slightly less juvenile version of "You would be mean, too, if . . ." I was like a mother defending her child's bad behavior—she missed her nap today; he had too much sugar—but in this case the bad behavior included manipulation, thievery, and murder. I wasn't justifying his crimes, but I wanted her to know that the Phantom was, well, mean for a reason.

I concede that the Phantom's transgressions are legion. As the Opera ghost, he extorts money from the theater managers. He deceives Christine into believing he has been sent by her dead father. He murders those who stand in his way as he attempts to control the young innocent he loves.

If there is anything redeeming about the Phantom, it is his musical genius; he has the voice of an angel and is a master composer. But even his ability to compose beautiful music is selfish, as he plans to finish the magnum opus he has poured twenty years into, place it alongside him in his coffin-bed, and "never wake up." It's not a gift if it dies with you, ungiven.

And yet the gifts that are given—to Christine by her father—are the very instruments Erik uses to spell her. The willful manipulation of a grieving daughter is perhaps the Phantom's most heinous crime.

Christine's father leaves her two gifts before he dies: his beloved violin, as faithful a companion to him as his own daughter, and a promise. The violin Christine gives back to him, allowing it to be buried with him in the little churchyard near where she and Raoul, the Phantom's rival, played as children. The music, her father, Raoul—all inextricably linked to Christine, a part of the natural flow of her life and history. And yet the Phantom, an outsider, unlinked, desecrates her father's grave to get at the sacred violin. As Christine visits her father's grave on the anniversary of his death, Erik plays the violin as a way to forge an unnatural connection to her. Christine's father's second gift is a promise, a promise to send the Angel of Music—an angel heard but not seen, a muse bestowing musical gifts, the stuff of his bedtime stories to her—when he died. This, too, the Phantom exploits, presenting himself to her as the Angel of Music, teaching her to sing from behind the mirror in her dressing room, the self-proclaimed "trapdoor lover," using his gift of illusion and magic to wedge his way into Christine's life story as if he fit there.

Somehow he knows these gifts, given in passage, have meaning, but he doesn't understand why, because he doesn't understand the nature of giving.

He doesn't understand that gifts are given free of strings, without compensation or expectation. When he gives Christine a gold ring—also a promise—he warns her: "I give you back your liberty so long as you wear the ring. As long as you keep it, you will be protected against danger and Erik remains your friend. But woe to you if you lose it, for Erik will have his revenge!"[4]

It's less a gift than a leash. A protective talisman, a false liberty. How can he determine whether or not she is free? How can she unmarry the man who is not her husband?

Everything in Erik's life is predicated on his delusion that he can control others for his own purposes. "I am a trapdoor lover," he says. "I can open and shut what I please."

This was the man I was defending to a stranger in my friend's kitchen.

"You would be mean, too," began my litany, "if . . ."

Your father left home in horror when he saw your infant face, more like a death mask than the face of a newborn, the countenance of a living corpse.

"If . . ."

Your mother stayed but made a tiny mask for you so that she didn't have to look at you. (This moment is precisely and painfully articulated in the musical when the Phantom sings, "This face, which earned a mother's fear and loathing; a mask, my first unfeeling scrap of clothing."[5])

"If . . ."

To spare your mother—who denied you even a single kiss— you ran away from home and survived by living in traveling freak shows, your unmasked face the star attraction.

"If . . ."

As you dwelt in the home you had made for yourself in the cellar of the Opera House, you fell in love with a beautiful young soprano named Christine, who performed above, and would do anything to make her love you.

"If . . ."

A young man with "a charming way about him," as different from you as possible ("blue eyes and the complexion of a girl"), returned from Christine's past and ruined everything.

"If . . ."

You were alone in your cellar with Christine and Raoul, and she had to choose between being your wife and saving the life of her true love and the lives of the hundreds of opera goers above. And you realized that "opening and shutting what you please" was the only way you would get her hand in marriage, because after all, how could she love you with that face?

My Own Mask

I am learning something as I go along, something I didn't bargain for when I started: what the red thread asks of you in return for binding you to the stories of others. It's not exactly a Faustian bargain, but something of your soul, if not bought and paid for, is greatly altered in the process. The carpet's torn away, a slat in your internal flooring is pulled up, dislodging nails and splitting wood, as a hand gropes below in the dirt and muck for any vulnerability, any tender spot that might connect you with the other person and his story. Empathy—literally "in feeling"—requires that the pain be shared.

I find that I am unexpectedly "in feeling" with the Phantom. The grief that awakens the senses can also revive past pain, drawing me back to a time in my life when I felt the most like him.

I didn't have a disfigured face, but I did have a disfigured body. Not from an accident or a handicap or a birth defect, but from hurtling into puberty before I was ready. I wasn't as much disfigured as overly figured. I know the immense pain adults feel who have been overweight as children (my friend Fred Rogers was one), but there is something more unsettling still about being overweight in such an obvious way, for obvious reasons. You're thrust upon, assaulted from within. There's no way to hide *that* under a mask.

That I stood out sorely in the midst of my five petite sisters was doubly cruel, even without thick lenses poking through the wire rims of my glasses or a mass of natural curls cut into a perfectly symmetrical circle atop my head. Nearsighted, ugly, and fat.

"Amy was a beautiful baby," my dad used to say, and maybe that's because it was the last time he remembered me being so.

During the last week of his life—after he had stopped talking—I was keeping vigil in his living room, where his hospital bed was set up. One morning I apologized for my couch-flattened hair and smeared mascara: "Sorry I don't look so pretty right now, Dad." He winked back as if to say, "Yes, you do." I left the room in tears. That was all I ever wanted from my father. It's what every little girl wants from her father: for him to think she is pretty.

In the awkwardness and insecurity of my teenage years, I immersed myself in the one thing I was good at, academics, in the same way the Phantom plunged himself into music. My older sister, whose prettiness afforded no such need, once sniped at me, "Books are your only friends."

That was true for a time. There is a natural tendency to hide from people when you think you're unbearable to look at, but after a while you become lonely in your cellar and long to be connected. That's when you get industrious.

I learned to tame the locks with a blow dryer and replaced the glasses with contact lenses, but the roundedness of my body required something more drastic—starvation diets that set off a nine-year battle with anorexia. (You can't look like a twelve-year-old boy without a fight.)

So when the red thread tied me to the Phantom, it did not give me a subtle reminder of our similarities but forced me to feel them again. For a time I walked around in the awkward body of my teenage self, looked out through the thick glasses again, felt the desperate need to hide in shame.

I tried to deny what was happening, masquerading it as some sort of existential lesson a writer needs to learn. In my journal I wrote:

In "opening myself vulnerably" (L'Engle) to this book I am also allowing access to other vulnerabilities, exposing other vulnerabilities, which helps explain some of my emotional distress while writing this chapter, especially a chapter about self-loathing, which opens up for me a time in my life when I was most pained by this kind of thinking, believing. I feel like the Israelites rebuilding the wall. I need to work with one hand and keep a sword in the other.

Who was I kidding? The red thread had knocked the sword right out of my hand.

I was defenseless and vulnerable. In pain. "In feeling."

Beneath the Mask

When my son was four, he had a phrase for bad characters who change stripes during the course of the story, penitents who ranged from Ebenezer Scrooge to Heidi's grandfather. He would say they "become good at the end." Whenever we began reading a new book or watching a new movie that included a villainous character, he would ask, "Do they become good at the end?" Sometimes they did; sometimes they didn't. If the Phantom is among those who do, how does it happen?

In the musical—Andrew Lloyd Webber's embellishment of Gaston Leroux's embellishment—we are led to believe it is a climactic kiss delivered by Christine. The stage directions from the libretto state its intention plainly: "Now calmly facing him, she kisses him long and full on the lips. The embrace lasts a long time. Raoul watches in horror and wonder."[6] But in Leroux's retelling, it is Christine's tears that set the Phantom free.

"She came to me with her beautiful eyes open," the Phantom recalls of that day.[7] That day in the cellar, he explains, Christine agrees to be his wife, and he spares Raoul. Then Christine comes to him with her beautiful eyes open, and in gratitude for Raoul's life, she tilts her forehead toward him ever so slightly.

He kisses her on the forehead, his first kiss, and begins to cry, falling at her feet. Soon Christine's tears begin falling too: "They trickled under my mask . . . and they mingled with mine. I tore off my mask so as not to lose one tear . . . and she did not run away! She wept with me."

Her tears, it seems, laid claim, flowed baptismally, seeped into his pores. They ran between his lips until the ugliness that lay beneath the skin, in his warped and rotted soul, was slowly washed away.

That's when I first realized what the dragon in the Phantom had been calling out for, what the helpless being in him needed. He needed to be connected to another living being. The mingling of Christine's tears with his was the first natural connection in his life.

And its impact is immediate: he releases her to Raoul, giving her the gold ring as a wedding present. He asks only one thing: that she bury him with the gold ring when he dies.

He knows she will be back soon, because her departure will kill him.

The Other Half

Recently, in my hometown, a tragic accident claimed the lives of four men when their single-engine plane crashed as they were returning from a college basketball game at the pilot's alma mater.

All were husbands and fathers who had made important contributions to the community, and their deaths were deeply felt even by those who didn't know them. Each of the four widows attended the funerals of the other widows' husbands, all held the same week.

The newspaper reported that during that mournful week, an unlikely discovery had been made. The widow and children of the pilot had visited the crash site, and there among the wreckage, the widow had expressed her desire to find her husband's wedding ring, realizing it was wishful thinking.

The widow's brother returned to the site and combed the area with a metal detector but found nothing. And then, in the last place he scanned, within five feet of the wooden cross erected by loved ones in memory of the men, the detector's signal went off. After digging a small hole, the brother stuck a knife deep into the ground, and when he pulled it out, it had wedged its way into the center of the wedding ring. At the pilot's funeral, the pastor noted that the wedding ring "was the one thing [the family] really wanted to find."[8]

The wedding ring was important to them because of what it symbolized. Symbols only work if there is a connection—a paternal violin that comforts, an angel of music promised from bedtime stories, a wedding ring that vows to love till death do us part. A symbol stands for something else by reason of relationship. The Greek word *sumbolon* means literally a token of identity that can be confirmed by comparing its other half. A wedding ring is exactly that—it identifies that you are part of someone else, that person's other half.

That was the Phantom's gift of passage. He knew losing Christine would cause his death. "I am dying of love," he says, and he does. But first he gives Christine the wedding ring—no longer a leash, it is a gift of freedom to marry Raoul, a release from Erik's spells, an escape from his trapdoors. He is able to give a gift because, for the first time in his life, he has a connection through which giving becomes possible. He has learned—and now I know—that gifts of passage are meaningful because of what they symbolize, and that symbols grow from relationships of love.

As with her father's beloved violin, Christine returns the gift to the Phantom, placing it on his finger to be buried with him. The Phantom dies a part of someone else.

It is the same ring found on the skeleton in the cellars of the Paris Opera House. "It was his skeleton," Leroux wrote. "I did not recognize it from the ugliness of his head. Everyone is ugly when dead for so long. I recognized it from the plain gold ring he wore. Christine Daaé had certainly slipped it on his finger when she came to bury him as she had promised."[9]

The Phantom is no longer identified by his ugliness but by a gold ring. No longer a dragon, he is now beautiful and brave.

Beautiful, my Dad's wink had said.

Both the Phantom and I had been freed from our cellars. He "became good at the end." He became a person—not a ghost or a monster or even a literary device—capable of sacrifice, worthy of forgiveness and redemption.

No wonder I felt heaven.

Chapter 5

THE LAST THING

The other day I dreamed that I was at the gates of heaven, and St. Peter said, "Go back to Earth. There are no slums up here." In anger I said, "Very well, I will fill heaven with slum people; then you will be forced to let me in."

—MOTHER TERESA

FROM WHAT I can see through the diamond-shaped gaps in the fence, the line is being held up by one little girl who is refusing to jump.

The swim teacher, a teenage girl, tries to coax the young swimmer into the water, where she stands ready to catch. The little girl bends forward tentatively, then sits down and tries to slide off the edge of the pool. The teacher won't allow the shortcut.

"It's so fun," the teacher offers. "You'll like it."

The little girl shakes her hands nervously at her side.

"You can *do* it," the teacher pleads and, waist-deep in the water, moves a little closer.

The indecisive little girl makes the decision to take herself out of the line, and the other kids, in single file, jump into the water one after another.

"Wasn't that fun?" the teacher asks. All the other kids say yes.

"Who wants to go again?" All the other kids raise their hands.

The little girl, shame-red, slides back into the line. She bends forward again, preparing to jump. Perhaps gravity will make her difficult decision for her. But before it can, she stands back up.

"Take a deep breath."

Suddenly—or finally—there is a splash in the water, and a mother claps in joy and relief. The little girl gets out of the water and hugs one of the little boys in line. She is now one of them; part of that elite corps of six-year-olds who can jump into the pool by themselves.

She gets back in line. When her turn comes around again, she hesitates. Then shakes her head no.

"You can do it," the teacher begins again.

I had witnessed a similar scene the day before, from behind the chain-link fence where all the mothers sit while their kids learn to swim. This time it was my daughter, Emily, in a different group of swimmers, who needed coaxing. She was older than this little girl, but her fear was also of jumping—this time into the yawning chasm they called "the deep end." All the laws of physics could not persuade her that she would eventually rise to the top.

Emily's teacher had also tried coaxing from the water, thankfully without enlisting the other children as cohorts. After my daughter refused several times, the teacher suddenly pulled herself out of the pool, came alongside my daughter, held her hand, and jumped into the deep end with her. Together they rose to the top. The next time—and every time after that—Emily was able to jump on her own.

It wasn't pressure that left the lasting impression; it was *presence*.

No one should have to do difficult things alone. The cause of the Phantom's death, his broken heart over Christine, is also the very thing that makes his death bearable. He dies knowing that he is connected to another living being; "I have tasted all the happiness the world can offer!" he cries out before his death. His communion with Christine, forged through mingled tears—she *empathizes* with him—means he doesn't die alone. The gold ring is proof of her presence.

But sometimes a gift of presence is more tangible still, like someone coming alongside who is willing to grab your hand, knowing you're afraid of the deep end.

GODFORSAKEN

My husband, Jeff, was feeling like a stranger in a strange land.

He hadn't spent four years in seminary, interminably parsing sentences in Greek and Hebrew, to pastor a flock of twenty-five in a town of one hundred. While we were in graduate school, we had attended large churches—megachurches—and his first post after graduation had been to a church six hundred strong. His next post had been to a smaller church, still with a respectable two hundred–plus members, but he had a greater role, greater responsibilities. When he left that church, we spent four months searching and praying, and this was where we landed—in a small church that sat at the crossroads of a town without a traffic light.

A city girl, I welcomed the church bells at noon, the small

country store, the plentiful wildflowers to arrange in vases around a parsonage so old the floors dipped from wear. But my husband struggled; this was not what he would have chosen. He appreciated a quieter life, too, but saw the reason for the stillness: an exodus from the town had left it lifeless. Buildings were hollowed out and abandoned, with only their faces still showing, like the movie set of an old Western, like ghosts in a ghost town. It's hard to save the world when the world lives someplace else. The place had been forgotten, godforsaken.

But he trudged on, preparing sermons with the same focus and purpose as if he were preaching to the multitudes. And then one day someone asked him to do something routinely ministerial, of seeming inconsequence: visit a sick farmhand in the hospital. Dutifully, my husband put on his tie and drove the forty-five minutes to the nearest hospital. That's where he met Junior for the first time.

Was Junior the victim of disappointed dreams too? Or had his life turned out exactly as he had expected? We didn't know much about him, so it was hard to tell.

My husband only knew that he occasionally worked for a farmer in our church (the farmer, not Junior, had requested the visit) and had suffered a mild stroke. When Jeff walked into the hospital room, he caught Junior thumbing through a Gideon's Bible—the last thing you'd want an uninvited preacher to catch you doing.

But Junior was thankful to be caught. And Jeff was grateful for the icebreaker. If not for the work of a faithful Gideon, who deposited the Bible in Junior's nightstand, Jeff might have cut the visit short. It would have been easy to be put off by Junior's rugged exterior, the deep-set grooves (etched from wear) that made his face look older than its fifty-seven years, the slightly vacuous stare. Instead, Jeff picked up the Gideon's Bible and saw past all that to something in Junior's eyes that begged him to stay.

Junior lived alone in the woods and wasn't used to company.

It's almost trendy now to long for the monastic life, to escape the din of modern living. Abbeys are opening their doors to those of us who want to hole up for a weekend and live in the quiet of a sparse cell, free from the distractions of computers and cell phones. I scheduled a long weekend away myself, to attend vespers with the nuns in the woods of Maryland, but had to cancel when a work event at a swanky hotel was scheduled the same weekend. "I have to buy a dress with sequins," I complained to the nun on the other end of the phone when I called to cancel, "but I'd rather be with you."

"I know, dear," she said. "Come back when you can." I haven't yet.

But flirting with monastic asceticism is different from what Junior's life was like. Being a hermit wasn't a vacation for him—or even a vocation, in the way it was for modern-day monk Thomas Merton, who petitioned his religious order for years to live by himself in the woods so he could pray and write in solitude.

I wondered if the word *hermit* always carried with it a religious connotation, and when I checked, I found that while the word means "living in the desert" (like the revered desert fathers), it is derived from the word *desolate*. That comes closer to describing what Junior's life was like. It was desolate, godforsaken.

He was raised by an uncle, but no one in town knew why his mother and father weren't there to care for him. When the uncle became ill, Junior nursed him until his death and then lived alone in the old house where he was born—a slanted house with dirt floors and no indoor plumbing. It was aged and worn, like Junior. Had he been the product of hard living, or the victim of a hard life?

My first impression of Junior was different from my husband's, when a week later he showed up unexpectedly at our home. I opened the front door, and there he stood, drawn up to his full height of six feet two inches, in coveralls splattered by mud and blood. My husband wasn't there to identify him; otherwise, he might have pointed out that the blank stare was a sign of the stroke, and the strange attire and sweat-soaked hair meant Junior had been hunting that morning. Without an interpreter, I was left with images from every horror film I'd ever seen. My eyes searched for the hidden ax; my ears listened for the whir of a chain saw. The blood dripping between his fingers did nothing to allay my fears.

There was tentative movement as Junior reached across the threshold of the parsonage to hand me the gift he was bearing: fresh-cut deer meat, his morning quarry.

I don't remember what happened next, whether either of us even spoke. I might have managed a thank-you. I only know I stood frozen in relief when Junior turned to walk away, frozen and holding the dripping meat he had seen fit to give us in thanks for the company.

The Little Flower

Agnes's life started out much like Junior's, albeit on the other side of the world. Her father was murdered when she was a child, and she never saw her mother and sister after her eighteenth birthday. Like Junior, she never married, never had children.

But she was not desolate. Her father's death was a dark tragedy in her childhood, but it was her choice, in acquiescence to a higher calling, to leave her mother and her sister. It was with similar resolve that she determined never to marry. And although childless, she was surrounded by myriad loved ones when she died; her final words were offered to her "dearest children."

Two similar beginnings, two divergent paths.

If you were to ask Agnes why her life and Junior's turned out so differently, she might have said that although much of the world is plagued by poverty, the United States has it worse, since its poverty is largely spiritual. As an example, she would point to our elderly, relegated to nursing homes, always looking longingly to the door, hungry for company. They never smile. Yet even the poorest in India smile, even while they're dying, she would say, because she knows. She had spent her life with them, offering them her presence. And because she cared so generously for them, they called the childless woman *mother*—Mother Teresa.

Agnes chose Teresa as her namesake when she took her religious vows because Thérèse de Lisieux, a nineteenth-century mystic known as the Little Flower of Jesus, was a proponent of doing little things with great love. "Great deeds are forbidden me," the Little Flower once wrote. "The only way I can prove my love is by scattering flowers, and these flowers are every little sacrifice, every glance and word, and the doing of the least actions for love."[1]

It's easy to see the Little Flower's influence on Mother Teresa, who, when awarded the esteemed Nobel Peace Prize, asked that the six thousand dollars allotted for the banquet in her honor be instead given to the poor in Calcutta. Mother Teresa was asked, upon accepting the award, "What can we do to promote world peace?" She answered, "Go home and love your family."

Inspired advice, but what if you're like Junior and you have none?

THE TRADE

Junior's visit to our home was followed by several others, much less frightening in nature. He and my husband had connected in the hospital over that Gideon's Bible sitting on his lunch tray. When Jeff opened it and read from it—"For by grace are ye saved through faith; and that not of yourselves: it is the gift of God" (Eph. 2:8 KJV)—Junior's eyes were wet with tears. There was no pressure, no coaxing from the water for Junior to jump in, just a gentle coming alongside. Jeff had brought Junior good news (*the* good news), and that had made him very grateful.

Junior showed his gratitude by continuing to drop off gifts. During one of his visits, he brought us a box of potatoes from his vegetable garden, one of the ways he made his living. He was concerned about me because I had missed church—he was now part of our small flock—due to illness the Sunday before. Most of the time when he talked to me, his gaze stayed fixed on the floor, but today he slowly raised his eyes to meet mine. "I remember you in my prayers," he said softly, without looking away.

Junior was praying for me, and now we, too, are connected.

We had asked Junior to spend Christmas Day with us but didn't know if he would take us up on the invitation. We knew he would feel comfortable with our family of four, but we were unsure he would want to be around our extended family, which pushed the guest list into double digits. A knock on the door came in the early afternoon, and there was Junior, standing on our front porch, all gussied up. Gone were the coveralls and work clothes; in their place he wore light blue seersucker pants, too thin for the winter air. Over his brightly patterned red and blue shirt, he wore a dark tweed jacket, his long arms stretching out beyond the too-short sleeves. He had carefully parted his hair, smoothing it down over his forehead, with one stray piece that refused to be tamed. I later wondered where he got the jacket, aged and worn and too small for his frame. Perhaps it had once belonged to the uncle who raised him; maybe his father had left it behind.

Junior had dressed up for our sakes.

I took a photograph of him that day. In it he is sitting, hands clasped, legs crossed in a chair in our living room, the sides of his mouth turned up in a reluctant grin. Several months later someone would give us three more photographs of Junior: two black-and-white photos from his childhood and one color photo of him as an adult. As far as I know, it is the whole of his family photo album, even though he is the only one in each of the pictures. I cherish these photos, but my favorite is still the one from Christmas Day. It's not because he traded his muddy coveralls for a tweed jacket, but because he traded being alone for being with us.

Friend, Move Up Higher

Mother Teresa was constantly surrounded by death, and perhaps that's why she respected life so much.

The wonder-worker of Calcutta and her sisters once found a man dying in the streets, his waxen body being eaten by worms. They took him to shelter, put him in bed, and carefully cleansed his body of parasites.

"I have lived like an animal in the street, but I am going to die like an angel, loved and cared for," he said as he laid his head on the clean sheets and closed his eyes for the last time.[2]

How a life ends is important, even if for just moments the person feels loved and cared for, connected.

When it was Mother Teresa's time to die, she filled her last moments carefully. She could have talked of her lifelong devotion to the poor, or reminisced about the family she left behind in her native land, or passed the mantle of her life's work on to someone else. Instead, she talked of the Little Flower, her namesake, who had just been made a Doctor of the Church. "Can you imagine," she said excitedly, "for doing little things with great love, the Church is making her a Doctor, like Saint Augustine!" Mother Teresa equated the Little Flower's promotion to Jesus' parable of the wedding feast, in which the guest who takes the lowest seat is approached by the host, who insists, "Friend, move up higher" (Luke 14:10 NASB). Like the wedding guest, the Little Flower was being honored for her humility, for doing little things. Mother Teresa underscored that very humility by honoring the Little Flower as she *herself* died. With both words and deeds, she fulfilled her final exhortation: "So let us keep very small and follow the Little Flower's way of trust and love and joy."

These words she spoke and dictated in a letter she addressed to her "dearest children."

Her last words may have been meant for her fellow sisters,

those under the auspices of her ministry, but they applied to all her dearest children—including the forsaken man being eaten by worms—she had nurtured spiritually.

The prophet Isaiah cried:

"Sing, O barren woman,
   you who never bore a child;
burst into song, shout for joy,
   you who were never in labor;
because more are the children of the
   desolate woman
than of her who has a husband,"
   says the LORD.
                              —Isaiah 54:1

Isaiah was prophesying that an exiled, desolate Jerusalem, like a woman unable to conceive children, would one day be restored, transformed into a heavenly city, the Jerusalem that is above.

To be sure, every person Mother Teresa had fed, clothed, and held while he or she died was given to her as a child to a desolate woman. Those children were now waiting for her in the heavenly city that her kindness—her presence—had helped populate.

I have an image in mind of what Mother Teresa may have looked like as she passed into that eternal city, an image from another mother's deathbed. An elderly woman had awakened from a coma just before she died and, to the surprise of her family, reached out her arms as if she were being handed something. She cradled the something in her arms, smiled broadly, and passed away, her arms still surrounding what no one else could see.

The woman's son told how his mother had lost her first child just moments after the baby's birth.[3] She had gone on to have several more children, but those who witnessed her death believe that an old wound was being healed; the mother was being reunited with her firstborn child as a gift of presence in her death.

I imagine that as Mother Teresa called out to her "dearest children" in her final moments, she, too, reached out and gathered to herself the multitude of children she had conceived in her lifetime.

She went to heaven cradling them, reunited to those who had gone before her, her children in spirit.

It was in their presence that she died like an angel, loved and cared for.

THE RED THREAD'S DREAM

Recently I had a dream about Junior—the first time I can ever remember dreaming about him. The red thread was binding again, reaching back, reconnecting, choosing to work while I was at rest.

In the dream I am riding in the back of a pickup truck, surrounded by several other people. I indicate to the other passengers that we are nearing Junior's house, as if we are taking a tour of Hollywood homes. For some reason I am facing backward for the journey, as if the exact way to his house is to remain a mystery to me, like a blindfolded captive being transported to an undisclosed location. I only know we are nearing his house because of the landmarks we have passed.

When we arrive at Junior's, I'm struck by how much bigger and nicer his dream house is than his real house. We all pile out of the pickup truck and decide to go inside, although I tell the others that Junior is not going to be there because he is recovering from surgery. To my surprise, he *is* there, still dressed in a hospital gown (the last thing I ever saw him wear). He is well enough to walk on his own and invites us to sit on his couch with him. He is more gregarious in the dream than in real life, and his speech is more relaxed than I remember. He seems comfortable.

I'm not sure he knows I am there (I have not seen him for many years), when suddenly he points me out to the others. He tells them something about me, but his words, like the way to his home, are kept from me. When I awake, I can't remember them.

The dream occurs in the early morning hours, and I stay in it a long time, pulling the covers over my head and muting the alarm clock. I want it to last not only because it reunites me with Junior, but because of the overwhelming sense of peace it brings. As long as I stay in the dream, the peace lingers. It envelops me, makes me feel I am afloat. I hate to wake up from it; it holds me so still.

Junior's Gift

When Junior left our home early in the evening on Christmas Day, he complained of not feeling well.

When his health took a turn for the worse in the months that followed, we assumed there were residual problems from the stroke. He continued to attend our little church when he could, and Jeff encouraged him to be baptized. Junior never felt well enough to set a date until early Easter morning, when he called Jeff at dawn with the request to be baptized that very day. He had been reading the Bible we gave him for Christmas and saw, there in its words, the directive to be baptized. Our small congregation scurried to get the baptismal tank filled and readied, and on the day of Christ's resurrection, Jeff held on to Junior as he plunged deep into the water. Together they rose to the top.

Soon Junior began to experience pain in new areas of his body: the rib cage, back, and leg. By early fall, we found out why. Cancer of the esophagus had spread to his bones. He was moved into the hospital for pain maintenance, his only recourse.

Junior questioned his newfound faith. "Has God really forgiven my sins?" he asked during one of Jeff's visits to the hospital. "Is God punishing me for something?" Jeff had wrestled with the same question himself when he felt banished to the small town where Junior lived.

One Sunday evening Junior called Jeff at home from the hospital. "Please come and spend the night with me," he asked. "It's the last thing I'll ever ask of you."

I marvel at the courage it took for Junior to make this request. He would not have inconvenienced Jeff for the world, but now he was asking him to drive to the next town late at night, after a long day of services, not just for a visit but to spend the night. Jeff was unsure what to do. Junior's illness was likely to stretch out over months; he had only been diagnosed with cancer three weeks before. Could Jeff accommodate Junior's every request? But in truth, Junior had made only one.

In the end Jeff decided to go, back to the same hospital where he had first met Junior. Junior needed to be able to open his eyes and see he was not alone, even if Jeff was just sleeping in the chair next to his bed. For most of his life, Junior had shunned the company of others; now he was crying out for it.

"It's the last thing I'll ever ask of you," he had said, and two days later he died.

In one year's time, Jeff had prayed with Junior over a Gideon's Bible, baptized him on Easter Sunday, and performed his funeral service. The only family listed on the funeral card consisted of four distant cousins, and I don't even know if they were there among the small crowd gathered for the ceremony at his graveside. Perhaps it was one of them who handed us the childhood photos of him to keep. It's hard to recall things when grief first strikes you senseless.

What I do remember is that Junior was ready to die; he had told Jeff so at the hospital. "I am ready to go to Paradise," he said. Paradise, that heavenly city, the once-barren woman. The place you hate to wake up from, it holds you so still.

If we had wondered why Jeff had been kept very small, scattering little flowers instead of doing great deeds, we now had our answer. God had brought Jeff into obscurity because that's where Junior lived. But Junior didn't die there. He died a part of someone else.

But something more had happened. God, who was in that godforsaken place after all, had given Jeff—in his barrenness—a child.

And no one had to do difficult things alone.

A GIFT *from* MY FATHER FIGURE

Chapter 6

PENNIES FROM HEAVEN

*Please ask God for whatever you feel that you want, and
God will do what God feels is best for you and for everyone else
in the world. Sometimes that includes taking somebody to
heaven, and we can't understand it at times. But when we
get to heaven, we will understand it, and we'll know that
everything was for the best in God's view.*

—FRED ROGERS

(when I asked him on behalf of a child why her
grandmother died, even though she prayed for her)

I WAS CLEANING up my home office one afternoon in mid-January, along with the rest of the world who had resolved to reorganize and streamline their lives in deference to a new year. I have two obstacles to neatness. One is that I need visual reminders of what I am working on and want to remember, and because of that, I tend to be a piler. (If I want to develop a mental construct for something, it has to be in my field of vision, often, and since my office is the nucleus of our home, there are piles everywhere.) The second is that a certain length of time has to pass, a certain distance has to be created, before I will part with some things—even to tuck them away in a file or box or anywhere I can no longer see them.

As an example, on that particular afternoon, I found a plastic bag containing a Sunday edition of the *Pittsburgh Post-Gazette* from nearly three years ago; the pages were crisp and neatly pressed, with all the usual Sunday extras still tucked inside. I don't live in Pittsburgh, but I was there that weekend for Fred Rogers's memorial service and wanted to make sure I had the city's coverage of the event. That doesn't explain why I kept the sale papers or the next week's *TV Guide* (neither was usable to an out-of-towner then, much less three years later). I guess I thought preserving it intact would somehow preserve the sacredness of the event itself. Sharing the newspaper's plastic reliquary was one other item that toppled out when I shook its contents loose—a handkerchief. A used handkerchief.

It has been thirty years since I last saved a soiled handkerchief. I was twelve. My paternal grandmother, whom we called Dee Dee, had just passed away, and I was learning for the first time that sometimes what's best in God's view is taking grandmothers to heaven. My dad had lent me his handkerchief during the funeral, and I had cried my first real tears of grief into it. I never gave it back to him, and I never washed it. (I guess I thought preserving it intact would somehow preserve the sacredness of the event itself.) After the funeral, in reverse order, came the Irish wake in honor of Dee Dee's ancestral heritage. I had trouble reconciling the tears and mourning at the church with the subsequent free-flowing alcohol and celebratory dancing in my grandparents' basement. I remember seeing my grandfather stumble a little, grief and bourbon an unkind mix. I didn't have a mental construct for funereal partying, and I didn't want to see it in order to form one. I slipped out of the basement and into our wood-paneled station wagon, leaving aunts, uncles, and cousins behind, to cry in less festive surroundings. I wanted to write down how I felt, but I couldn't find any blank paper, so I turned over my science homework (the epidermal layer sketched with colored pencils on the road trip to my grandparents'; I must have been unhappy with how the hair follicle and subcutaneous layer came out, because the drawing had been discarded on the floorboard) and began writing. This is what I wrote:

And I remember my Dad, his sad and tear-stained face, walking slowly, but not hesitantly, toward the silver casket. I looked up from my sister's shoulder she had generously given me to lean on, in saddening comfort. He reached his hands and gently touched her hair, not trying to hold back any feelings. I heard his gentle shaking voice speak softly, and the words that were spoken brought tears to my eyes.

He stammered, "I'll see you later, Dee Dee; yeah, I'll speak to you later." His hand was slowly brought away, and I sensed the faraway look in his eyes. He turned his head away.

And I cried.

I still have those tears in Dad's handkerchief.

Sometime after we returned home, Dad was cleaning out the station wagon and discovered the message written on my science homework. He smoothed out the rumpled paper and did what he always did with my poetry and writing: he typed it up (all caps; he wasn't any good at typing), dated it—AMY, 10/10/74, AGE 12—and framed it.[1]

Some go to the typewriter, writes Frederick Buechner in *A Room Called Remember*:

> We are all of us more mystics than we believe or choose to believe. . . .We have seen more than we let on, even to ourselves. Through some moment of beauty or pain, some sudden turning of our lives, we catch glimmers at least of what the saints are blinded by; only then, unlike the saints, we tend to go on as though nothing has happened. . . .
>
> Some, of course, go to the typewriter. . . . There are always some who have to set it down in black and white.[2]

Dad knew that about me even then. It's just that now when grief strikes, I have to do my own typing.

A few years ago, Dad sent me a copy of my ode to Dee Dee (which, now that I read it again, is really an ode to him, to his grief) when he realized that I had inherited his need to preserve things intact. I read it aloud at his funeral. Now I understand the pain he was feeling that day, saying good-bye to a parent. Now I know why he touched her hair, talked to her even though she couldn't hear him.

"It's sad when our daddies die. Makes us one less person inside," said a character in Pamela Ribon's first novel.[3]

That was it exactly. I was one less person inside: the person who lent me his handkerchief, who set my words down in black and white.

When I first met Fred Rogers in 1994, I didn't know that he would become like a father to me. Most people assume that if you need a father figure, you must not have had a very good one to start with.

I have been asked many times the reason Fred and I became friends (isn't it every kid's dream to become Mister Rogers's real-life "neighbor"?), but predicting friendship is an imprecise science. I've had other brushes with celebrity. I went to college with Michael Jordan when he was part of Carolina's dream team, and Jack Nicklaus Jr. was also a classmate. I have a letter from Richard Nixon typed on White House stationery and a postcard from humorist Dave Barry. When I worked in TV, I interviewed C. S. Lewis's stepson and Manson family member Tex Watson (in an unsanctioned phone call from prison). I once left a message on David Cassidy's answering machine. None of these luminaries became my friend.

It must have been what happened before Fred and I met that laid the groundwork for our friendship. I was working in television and decided to ask him for an interview as an extension of some children's programming our team had done over the summer. I wasn't a fan of his show growing up, but he captured my two-year-old's attention so readily and completely that soon he had mine too. It's easy to judge someone by prejudices, to rely on parodies to form your opinion—it's much easier than doing your homework—but it never does justice to the real person.

I didn't know at the time that Fred Rogers rarely gave interviews, and so when weeks passed without a response to my request,

I didn't get worried. I just used the time to get to know him better, continuing to watch *Mister Rogers' Neighborhood* every day with my toddler. The more I watched, the more my adolescent prejudices of Mister Rogers began to fade away, prejudices that masked the real person underneath all the making-fun-of. I had this in mind one afternoon when I opened my local newspaper and saw an op-ed piece deriding him. I was offended that the syndicated columnist had lumped Fred together with a group of self-esteem gurus who believe any praise—including empty praise—helps a child to grow. Mister Rogers didn't belong in that group. What upset me was that the writer never bothered to find that out. Instead, he dismissed Fred's life work as "psychobabble."

I wrote the columnist a letter, gathering up a group of facts (something he had neglected to do) to prove him otherwise. I concluded with a "shame on you" for wasting his bluster on someone who was doing something positive for my kids. I sent the op-ed piece and a copy of my response to Fred's office, thinking the staff should know this column was in print. I didn't find out until I got to Pittsburgh that that was the thing that convinced Fred I was sincere enough to be trusted. That letter, of all things, clinched the interview.

"Amy did her homework," Fred said to an associate just after I left Pittsburgh. That's what earned his trust; that's what made us friends.

PENNIES FROM HEAVEN

I have a collection of pennies on my desk in my home office; they have their own separate pile. Most of them I've found on my daily walks around the neighborhood, but others hail from such exotic places as the sticky floors of Chicago O'Hare Airport. I started collecting them (and by collecting I mean picking them up off the ground when I find them) after Fred died.

I associate pennies with Fred Rogers because on my second trip to his neighborhood, he told me the story of a little boy who had asked him how he had gotten on all the pennies. The lad had mistaken the Lincoln Memorial for the Neighborhood trolley, which runs from Mister Rogers' television house to the Neighborhood of Make-Believe and back again. (It does look just like the trolley.) And since the trolley was on one side, the little boy deduced Mister Rogers was the man in profile on the other side. So I pick them up and keep them because they remind me of Fred.

Recently I found out that Fred had a penny association himself. His father had a "habit, this wonderful habit" (as Fred called it) of leaving pennies on windowsills. Even when he came to New York City to help young Fred, who had just landed his first television gig as an assistant producer, find a place to live, he carried his habit with him. As they walked along the streets of the Big Apple, Fred's father stopped to leave pennies on windowsills. "Why do you do that, Dad?" Fred asked, a little embarrassed.

"I just like to think of the people who will be finding them," his father said.[4]

I don't literally think Fred drops pennies from heaven as his father intentionally left them on windowsills, but it does make me think of him, remember him. He always thanked me in his letters and phone calls for "remembering him."

"For as long as you remember me, I am never entirely lost," begins another insightful reflection from Frederick Buechner, to whose work Fred introduced me. "When I'm feeling most ghost-like, it's your remembering me that helps remind me that I actually exist."[5]

In fact, it was remembering Fred that led to my writing about him.

I had just returned from his memorial service in Pittsburgh, and I was sitting on my back porch thinking about a story he had shared with me just a few months before he died.

It was about an elderly woman who had lived near him in his small hometown, the kind with back porches and neighbors speaking over fences. He was five years old at the time, and he often visited Mama Bell—that's what everyone called her—when he needed a snack. He would arrive on her back porch, which led into her kitchen, and wait for her to ask if he had come for toast sticks. One afternoon, to Fred's surprise, Mama Bell asked if he would like to make his own. She superintended as he put the bread in the toaster, spread butter and jam on it, then sliced it into four narrow sticks. Fred, who liked to put his emotions into words, felt two things that day: implicit trust from Mama Bell and grown-up pride in himself.

Not long after that afternoon together, Mama Bell got sick and died. Fred wondered, many years later, if Mama Bell knew she was dying. Was she teaching him to make his own toast sticks because she wouldn't be around to make them anymore? She must have sensed that after she was gone, it would be a source of comfort to him. A simple legacy, surreptitiously given, slipped in through Mama Bell's back door.

While I was sitting on my back porch, trying to put my own emotions into words, it occurred to me that Fred had done the same thing with me, only the toast sticks he had left me were spiritual in nature—lessons and insights gleaned from our letters, phone calls, and visits in the neighborhood. Spiritual toast sticks.

Those three words dropped into my mind—like pennies from heaven—and became the genesis of a book I wrote to honor Fred and to share what he had taught me: *The Simple Faith of Mister Rogers: Spiritual Insights from the World's Most Beloved Neighbor.*

Some go to the typewriter.

Many who have read the book have told me it made them cry. In fact, many of those admissions came from men. (One male interviewer indicated to me during a break that he wanted to edit his tears out of our radio interview, but he knew Fred wouldn't have wanted that.) That the book evokes emotion is not surprising to me, since it was part of my grieving process to put into words the impact of our nine-year friendship. But there was something else at work there, something readers didn't know. Nine days after I met with my publisher about the book idea, my dad coughed up blood. During the months I wrote the book, he was dying. I made eight trips to Ohio during the time he was sick; one trip, in mid-May, was to say good-bye. The doctor said it might be two hours or two weeks, but he would not survive the latest setback. The doctor was wrong, and after ten emotionally exhausting days at Dad's bedside in hospice, I flew back home. Back to the typewriter. Savvy readers can tell you when that happened, when the tenor of the book changed. From that point on, my pain was pressed into every word. I finished the book a month before Dad died. He only saw the book cover, never read a word of it. He did know it was dedicated to him.

If Dad was jealous of Fred, he never said so to me. During his last days, though, when he could still talk, and he was seeing his father and Dee Dee and others who were already in heaven, he told me Fred was among them. He said it bothered him that Fred was interrupting his time alone with his daughter. "He's a snoop," Dad said, then cussed like the sailor he had been. "Please don't cuss in front of Mister Rogers," I joked, but maybe that's how he felt about his daughter writing a book about a father figure instead of a father.

I think he would have known when the tenor of the book changed. He would have known that he was pressed into every word.

———

It didn't occur to me until I began to search for the meaning of my father's dying gift that what I had used as a spiritual analogy in *The Simple Faith of Mister Rogers* was in fact a tangible gift that Mama Bell had bequeathed a young Fred Rogers. Teaching him to make toast sticks on his own was her gift of passage to him. Through the gift, she formed in his young mind not only what it means to be a true neighbor but what it means to give someone exactly what he needs to heal after you're gone.

It was God's way of "helping him understand," just as Billy's father said when he saw the red fern growing up out of the makeshift grave.

Now many months into my search, I am being issued a new challenge: to take what I've learned so far and use it to discern the gift Fred Rogers left me. Even though I lost my father figure a year before my actual father, I had never tried to seek out Fred's gift to me. Before my father's death, I didn't understand that gifts were given. I didn't understand that a grieving person is not left empty-handed. Dad's death revealed the existence of gifts of passage to me, and through the filter of my newly awakened senses, I now turn back to look at my first paternal loss.

Up until this point there has been some distance between the other stories and me. Though I was deeply moved by the stories of Jack and Joy, Gina and John, and Erik and Christine (and was even willing to revisit my own grief over Junior), this is different: Fred was like a father to me. No more a distant teacher who visits my dreams, the red thread now wants to draw uncomfortably close, to comfort what's most tender, both to tear and to heal. It had bound me to Fred Rogers a decade ago, but now it tightens, pulls me in closer to see the gift he left me as he died.

"When you remember me," Buechner wrote, "it means that you have carried something of who I am with you, that I have left some mark of who I am on who you are."[6]

Everyone needs tangible reminders, the evidence that some mark has been left. That's why I began picking up pennies after Fred died and why he made toast sticks on his own after Mama Bell died. It's why I now have two unwashed handkerchiefs in my collection. It's why I'm writing this book.

It is not to keep those we've lost from feeling ghostlike.

It is to keep ourselves from feeling that way.

LOVING YOUR NEIGHBOR, NOW AND FOREVERMORE

There has been some criticism of Fred, even since his death, that his emphasis on loving your neighbor was imbalanced. Too much acceptance, too much tolerance, some say. As his friend (and, as I've been dubbed by some reviewers, his spiritual biographer), I've borne the brunt of this criticism as well.

But the basis of Fred's understanding of what it means to love your neighbor came from his favorite seminary professor, Dr. William Orr. This is how he explained it to me:

> Evil would like nothing better than to have us feel awful about who we are. And that would be back in here [in our minds], and we'd look through those eyes at our neighbor, and see only what's awful—in fact, *look* for what's awful in our neighbor.
>
> But Jesus would want us to feel as good as possible about God's creation within us, and in here [in our minds], we would look through those eyes, and see what's wonderful about our neighbor. I often think about that.[7]

Fred saw the choice as a daily one: you can be either an accuser, like the evil one, or an advocate, like Jesus.

He saw me make the choice the day I shot off a letter to the op-ed writer, who had made his own choice.

What we do imperfectly here on earth, Fred reasoned, we will do perfectly in heaven.

"When I think about heaven, it is a state in which we are so greatly loved that there is no fear and doubt and disillusionment and anxiety. It is where people really do look at you with those eyes of Jesus."[8]

Philosopher and Boston College professor Peter Kreeft would agree. When asked if heaven will be boring, he responded with an answer that echoes Fred's sentiments:

There are only six things that never get boring on Earth . . . knowing and loving yourself, your neighbor, and God. Since persons are subjects and not objects, they are not exhaustible; they are like magic cows that give fresh milk forever. . . .

And in order to love we must know, get to know, as endlessly as we love endlessly. This never gets boring, even on Earth: getting to know and love more and more someone we already know and love. It is . . . preparation for our eternal destiny of infinite fascination.[9]

Endlessly getting to know and love God; endlessly getting to know and love our neighbor. The same task we have on earth.

We will spend eternity doing our homework.

⸻

One of the things Fred would be happy about is how many people I've met through writing a book about him. He was always trying to connect people. ("If you are ever in such-and-such a place, please call my friend so-and-so," he would say.) One of the people Fred inadvertently connected me to is a gifted young writer named Sam.[10]

Sam told me about a dream he had about Fred after he had "gone to heaven" (Fred's preferred way of saying "passed away"). In the dream, which felt more like a visitation to Sam (and smacks of the red thread to me), Sam was able to finally meet his iconic hero. Sam noticed that Fred didn't look like the grandfatherly man of his last days on TV, but a much younger version, like the black-and-white footage of him with slicked-down hair while he worked mostly behind the scenes for *The Children's Corner*, the forerunner to *Mister Rogers' Neighborhood*.

C. S. Lewis likewise imagines the rejuvenating effect of death when he explains what happens to King Caspian after he dies in *The Silver Chair*: "And the dead King began to be changed. His white beard turned to gray, and from gray to yellow, and got shorter and vanished altogether; and his sunken cheeks grew round and fresh, and the wrinkles were smoothed, and his eyes opened, and his eyes and lips both laughed, and suddenly he leaped up and stood before them—a very young man."[11]

Of course Lewis was writing fantasy, but is it possible we will be both free from boredom *and* young in heaven?

I turn again to Peter Kreeft: "Medieval philosophers usually thought we would all be 33, the ideal age, the age of maturity, as of Christ's earthly maturity. I take it this is symbolically accurate."

Interestingly enough, Fred was thirty-three years old during the last year of *The Children's Corner*.

"In Heaven," Kreeft continues, "no one will be old. Yet in a sense everyone will be both old and young, as a reflection of the God who is the Alpha and Omega, oldest and youngest."[12]

When Sam commented to Fred in his dream that he looked much younger now, Fred simply replied, "Yes, but I still have the same eyes."

I'm certain he does. Eyes that saw what was good about his neighbor on earth see perfectly what's good about his neighbor in heaven. Those eyes of Jesus.

Mama Bell's gift of passage to a young Fred Rogers became in turn a gift to me. It gave me the imagery to understand what he had passed along to me during our friendship. The fact that he first told me the story of Mama Bell just a few months before he died gives it special significance as well. Perhaps he knew the story would come to me while I was thinking about him, and I would see his gift of spiritual toast sticks as a sacred trust to share with others.

But I know now that wasn't his dying gift to me. It wasn't what he gave me as he was going to heaven.

That gift was a letter.

I didn't know Fred was dying when he wrote the letter. His stomach cancer was newly diagnosed, and it ravaged his body in weeks, just as bone cancer had ravaged Junior's. There were a few days, one of his staff later told me, when he was in the hospital and asked for his mail. He was able to dictate only a few letters before he became too weak to continue. He went home to die.

When his letter arrived, I was hurt by it. It was the only typed letter I had ever received from him. Gone was his perfect penmanship, the stroke of his blue pen, his personal stash of stationery. Instead, it was typed on *Mister Rogers' Neighborhood* letterhead, and someone else had written my address on the envelope. I was confused by the formality of it but relieved to see, at the close of the letter, his familiar script. It read: "Grace and Peace and Love to you all—Fred." In the letter he expressed his hopes for me in the new year and mentioned how much it meant to him that I was in his thoughts during the Christmas holidays. He expressed concern for the world and said what fine people my kids had grown into. When he died three weeks later, I understood why the letter had been typed.

Now I understand something more, after the time I've spent with my teachers in grief. They have taught me that gifts are not always obvious; sometimes you don't know where the seeds are planted until the red fern begins to push its way out of the soil. I've learned there are times when a gift *is* wrapped up in a neat little package—like a carefully written letter in a sealed envelope— but you've overlooked it, dismissed it as an afterthought. I know now that what is essential when you die is to feel connected to another human being. Most important, I learned that gifts of passage are meaningful because of what they symbolize: Fred Rogers had been a prolific letter-writer all of his adult life, and this, his close associate told me, was likely the *last* letter he ever wrote.

The thing that had caused me pain was now a singular treasure, because while he was dying, Fred Rogers remembered me.

Like Mama Bell, Fred knew he was dying and slipped his gift to me through the back door. He knew what was important to me. He knew what I needed to heal after he was gone.

Fred Rogers went to the typewriter. He took his gratitude for our friendship, his implicit trust in me, and he set it down in black and white.

GIFTS *of*
HONOR

Chapter 7

A HOME FOR MARY

And a sword will pierce your own soul too.

—SIMEON IN LUKE 2:35
(spoken to Mary on the day baby
Jesus was presented at the temple)

SOMETIMES GOD'S WILL for a son is to break his mother's heart.

That's what Father John was saying, his words rising above the insuppressible sounds that fill a church when someone loses a child.

Mary was forewarned. Simeon had told her when a newborn Jesus was presented at the temple that a sword would pierce her soul too.

But my friend Jean had no warning. There was nothing out of the ordinary about that morning until the bike her nine-year-old son was riding skidded out from his gravel driveway, across an invisible boundary, and into the road that ran in front of his house. The young woman driving the car had no time to stop.

Now Jean and her husband, Ed, were sitting in the front pew

at their only child's funeral, unable to take in what Father John was saying because of the sword piercing through.

Blessed Are They

The news of Jean's devastating loss first comes to me through a university e-mail. Since I'm not teaching this semester, I barely scan the message, unremarkable in plain text. Then I see Jean's name; then I read of Matthew's accident. Gone is the decorum of the telegram; in its place the death notice of a child is sent through cyberspace.

My sensibility toward grief is different now, and I think of what awaits Jean in the days ahead. I want to be able to "participate" in her grief with her, as Fred Rogers reminded me he often did with his friends: "To be able to participate in the life of someone who is in deep grief has been a great gift to me," he once told me. "Jesus said, 'Blessed are they who mourn.' He didn't say, 'Blessed are the people who comfort them that mourn.' He said, 'Blessed are they that mourn.' They definitely give gifts to those with whom they choose to be in their mourning."

I must have had this in mind when I fell asleep one night soon after Matthew's death and dreamed about Jean and me. In the dream we were standing near a lake, when suddenly I reached out for her hand, and we jumped into the water together. It is identical to my daughter's experience in the deep end of the swimming pool, except for the fact that that experience didn't occur for several more months. The dream anticipated it.

Jean and I sank down, down into the water until we hit the very bottom. I wondered if we would stay there motionless and let the water fill our lungs. Instead, Jean kicked hard at the lake's floor, and we rose to the surface intact.

Blessed are they who mourn, Jesus said. Then I realize I have missed something important—obvious, even—in my search to find the meaning of my dad's gift. If the seeds of the red fern— the genesis of gifts of passage—are birthed from eternity, if the spot where they are sown is sacred, then certainly there is much for me to learn by seeking the source of these gifts, the Author of eternity himself.

He, too, chose those with whom he wanted to be in his mourning. He, too, gave gifts.

A HOME FOR MARY

I find that John is the only gospel writer who tells me about Jesus' dying gift, given to his mother, on the day Simeon's words to her are fulfilled.

"Near the cross of Jesus stood his mother. . . . When Jesus saw his mother there, and the disciple whom he loved standing nearby, he said to his mother, 'Dear woman, here is your son,' and to the disciple, 'Here is your mother.' From that time on, this disciple took her into his home" (John 19:25–27).

Perhaps John is the only apostle to include the exchange because he is the only one who witnessed it. The shepherd had been struck, and all the sheep had scattered. John himself records Jesus' predicting this desertion. But if John had scattered initially, he must have come back, because there he is, at the cross. He reverses the parable of the lost sheep, in which the shepherd leaves the ninety-nine sheep to seek the one lost. Now the ninety-nine have scattered, and one sheep wanders back, in search of the shepherd.

Then, of course, John may have been the only one to write about the gift because he was "the disciple whom Jesus loved," and the gift involved him—was, in fact, him. John had been part of Jesus' inner circle during his life, and now with the three Marys—Mary, Jesus' mother; Mary the wife of Clopas; and Mary Magdalene—comprised the inner circle of his death.

How someone becomes part of death's inner circle is a mystery with an air of efficiency. Those who work with the dying believe they choose their inner circle at death—those with whom they choose to be in their mourning—as deliberately as they choose their inner circle during life. "If you are meant to be present at the time of death, you don't have to plan it; you will be," says a social worker who has spent years working with the dying.[1] Accounts abound of the dying who suspend their own death, waiting for a son or daughter or another loved one to arrive. And there are just as many accounts of family members who refuse to leave the bedside of the dying for days, refusing to eat or sleep, and then leave the room momentarily to answer the phone or the door, and the loved one dies.

It isn't necessarily a favorite who finds his or her way into death's inner circle. Calling himself the disciple whom Jesus loved does not mean John was Christ's favorite, only that he shared an especially close bond with him. (The fact, however, that he made the inner-circle cut both times is significant.) Sometimes it is someone with whom the dying has unfinished business; something has to be resolved, put to rest, or set in motion for the dying to have the closure needed for a peaceful death. An emotional or practical setting a house in order.

When Jesus says, "Here is your son," and "Here is your mother," he is, according to scholars, doing just that. He is not making a suggestion or a recommendation, but something "more like a testamentary disposition." A testamentary disposition refers to who gets what property after a person dies.

Jesus is making out his will.

"A crucified man," one scholar writes, "has the right to make testamentary dispositions, even from the cross. Jesus now makes use of this right, and with the official formula of the old Jewish family law he places his mother under the protection of the apostle John."[2]

Jesus bequeaths his mother to John (or John to his mother).

At the hour of his greatest anguish, he who is the fulfillment of all commandments keeps the fifth—the one commanding us to honor our mothers and fathers—until the end.

He sets his house in order by providing one for her.

CHARIOTS OF FIRE

One of the reasons John was considered part of Jesus' inner circle was because of the special access he was given into the most intimate moments of Jesus' life. John and his brother James (whom Jesus dubbed the Sons of Thunder, perhaps for an incident in which they suggested they call fire down from heaven as reproof for inhospitality) and Peter formed a strategic triad among Jesus' chosen twelve, with unusual opportunities and privileges during his earthly ministry.

John, James, and Peter, for example, are the only apostles Jesus allows to follow him to the house of Jairus, a synagogue ruler, where they witness his raising Jairus's daughter from the dead.

They are the three set apart to remain closest to Jesus at Gethsemane, the garden where he goes to pray before he is arrested and put to death. There they are the sole trustees of his most vulnerable of admissions: "My soul is overwhelmed with sorrow to the point of death" (Matt. 26:38)—the soul Simeon had declared thirty-three years before would be pierced with a sword. The directive was prophetic of Jesus first, then Mary "too."

It was Jesus' suffering that would cause Mary's. It was Matthew's inability to stop his skidding bike that would cause Jean's. Sometimes God's will for a son is to break his mother's heart.

But before Gethsemane, John, James, and Peter are also the only three present at the Transfiguration, where they witness Jesus on the mountaintop, suddenly changed so that "his face shone like the sun, and his clothes became as white as the light" (Matt. 17:2).

If that isn't staggering in itself, the glorified Jesus is joined on the mount by Moses and Elijah, dead men.

It's a mistake, though, to call Elijah a dead man. Elijah, the great Old Testament prophet, destined to be the restorer of all things, never died. It's not that he didn't make a passage from earth to heaven; it's just that he did so via a chariot of fire instead of the flames of a funeral pyre. He was "translated" or taken up to heaven without having to die first.

It is the passage itself that infuses gifts with special significance, enables ordinary gifts to offer extraordinary help. That gifts can offer supernatural aid is a theme central to biblical stories and to other stories as well. So central, in fact, that in most literature, receiving a gift is essential to the protagonist's completing his assigned task, fulfilling his destiny. In many cases, the hero encounters a helper, usually a sage old man, who imparts the gifts. Everyone has a divinely assigned task in real life, too, and is given gifts to accomplish that task.

Such is the case with Elisha, the attendant to the prophet Elijah. In his passage from one world to the next, Elijah leaves behind a mantle, a cloak that figures significantly into Elisha's first and last encounters with Elijah. When Elisha first appears in the Bible, he is out plowing in a field. Elijah approaches him and throws his mantle around Elisha's shoulders, thus signifying Elisha's divinely assigned task: to succeed Elijah as prophet.

No other account of Elisha is included in the Bible until Elijah is about to be taken to heaven, and again, the centerpiece of the account is the sage old prophet's mantle. Elijah, aware that it is his day to be taken to heaven in a whirlwind, travels to three cities to see the companies of prophets stationed there, and then crosses the Jordan River on dry ground, after striking and dividing the water with his mantle. Three times during the day's wanderings, Elijah tells his attendant Elisha to stay put, and three times Elisha doggedly refuses, determined to be in Elijah's inner circle until the end.

After the two cross the Jordan, Elijah asks Elisha, "What can I do for you before I am taken from you?"

Elisha responds, "Let me inherit a double portion of your spirit" (2 Kings 2:9).

Elisha is not being greedy but invoking inheritance law, just as Jesus was in essence making a legal transaction by providing for Mary's care. Elisha is asking for what is due the firstborn son: a double portion of the inheritance. While he was not Elijah's biological son, he was his spiritual son (as Junior was Jeff's), and that's what he asks for: spirit. Elijah tells him that his request will be granted only if Elisha sees his master being taken to heaven. (He may have been stating the biblical equivalent to "If you're meant to be present at the time of death, you don't have to plan it; you will be.")

Suddenly a chariot of fire driven by horses of fire appears, and Elijah is taken to heaven in a whirlwind. Elisha sees it all. It is the last time anyone would see Elijah on earth; that is, until John, James, and Peter unexpectedly encounter him on the mount with Jesus.

After tearing his own clothes in grief (separation is painful even when there is not a literal death), Elisha picks up the mantle that fell from Elijah as he disappeared from sight. (It is thought that the cloak was Elijah's only piece of clothing, in which case he left the world just as he came into it.)

The mantle is a visible sign, the tangible evidence that God has answered Elisha's request, giving him the very thing he needs to complete the work Elijah has started.

Elisha takes his gift and strikes the Jordan, and again it parts. A company of prophets who have gathered at the river see it divide and acknowledge the succession. Together they exclaim, "The spirit of Elijah is resting on Elisha" (2 Kings 2:15).

They are right, times two.

I wonder, as I read of Elisha's request and his invocation of inheritance law, what happens when you've lost your firstborn son and there are no other children to inherit your wealth or your spirit. You begin to wonder such things after your close friend loses her only child.

Perhaps the law works backward; instead of giving twice as much, twice as much is taken from you. If the deaths are reversed (child first, parent second), maybe the law is reversed as well. It's unnatural, a disruption in the expected order of things, to lose a child. If the child is an only child, there is a double blow, a sword that cuts twice as deep, a bargain that demands two pounds of flesh—because you can't be a mother without a child. Jean's husband, Ed, had grown children, not that his devastation in losing Matthew was any less. But he was, at least, still a father. Jean was different. "There was a mother; *a mother once*: among the weeping train," wrote Charles Dickens as he watched the funeral procession of a child.[3] Because Ed was much older than Jean, she had also lost the provision for her future, a son to take care of her in old age. Who was going to provide a home for *her*? It isn't a single-victim accident when neither mother nor son survives the crushing weight of an automobile that can't stop in time.

A SECOND SWORD

When Jesus honors his mother by assigning care of her to John and Elijah asks Elisha what he can do for him before he is taken to heaven, both are acting deliberately. Their provision for those left behind is intentional. But as I look beyond Jesus' gift and Elijah's gift to others in the Bible, I find not all gifts of passage are.

Some are not bestowed but wrenched.

We have a modern counterpart of this concept. If someone has something he really doesn't want you to have, he may jokingly concede that it may be yours someday, as in "when you pry it from my cold, dead hands." This is usually said in jest, during a battle over the television remote, a favorite coffee mug, or any other object of great attachment. It's meant to be hyperbole. No one takes it literally. But in the case of at least one biblical gift of passage, it fits.

The phrase essentially conveys how a young shepherd boy gets his hands on the gift he needs to continue in his journey, to complete the mission assigned to him. The boon isn't conferred by a wise old man but wrested from the hands of its unintended grantor. That the grantor's hands would be neither cold nor dead but for the shepherd's slingshot adds yet another dimension to the story.

The shepherd boy is, of course, David, the youngest son of Jesse, in the battle that has come to typify the age-old struggle between the underdog and the bully. Forgoing the armor and sword of King Saul in favor of a slingshot and five smooth stones from the stream, David defeats the nine-foot-tall Philistine named Goliath, who dares to "defy the armies of the living God" (1 Sam. 17:26). David is not a warrior; he is at the battlefield only because his father has asked him to bring grain, bread, and cheese to his three older, battle-worthy brothers. He is there to make a food drop. But he reaches the battle line just as Goliath issues the first of his twice-daily challenges to the armies of God, and David takes him up on it. When King Saul expresses doubt— David is only a boy—David declares that God has delivered him from the lion and the bear as he defended his sheep, and he will also deliver him from Goliath.

This he proves true when he dispatches Goliath with a stone to the forehead and the giant falls facedown on the ground.

Since David has no sword (and has refused Saul's), he disarms the fallen warrior and uses Goliath's own sword to cut off his head. The head goes to Jerusalem; the sword is tucked away in David's tent, his personal spoil of war.

The sword, an impressive weapon with an iron point that alone weighs fifteen pounds, is less gift and more plunder, but its future importance to David is as significant as Elijah's mantle, even though it is acquired under very difference circumstances.[4] It is a gift of passage in which the recipient himself is responsible for the "passage," which by a strange twist is what the name Goliath means.[5] The sword of Goliath is moved from David's tent to the tabernacle, perhaps because David wants to establish who the true Victor is.

David's conquest brings him great renown, and his victory is immortalized in verse by the women who greet him with dance and song at his homecoming: "Saul has slain his thousands, and David his tens of thousands" (1 Sam. 18:7).

Hebrew poetry allows for "thousands" and "tens of thousands" to mean essentially the same thing, to be used interchangeably, but King Saul sees only an unfavorable comparison and gets out his own weapon.

The next day, while David (shepherd, giant slayer, and musician) plays the harp to relieve Saul of an evil spirit, the king hurls a spear at him. Twice.

Unable to kill David, Saul sends him away on military campaigns, hoping someone else's aim is more accurate. David's continued success in battle only brings him more acclaim. Saul calls David back home for more harp playing and spear throwing. This time David runs away for good.

It is as dramatic a reversal of fortune as could beset the young David:

The bearer of provisions now has no bread.

The shepherd once certain of God's will doesn't know what to do next.

The victor in battle is now without a weapon.

The boy who faced a defiant giant is now running away from a cowardly king.

David arrives on the doorstep of the tabernacle in Nob and asks the priest Ahimelech for some bread. He tells the priest that his lack of food is due to the urgency of the mission the king has sent him on (and there is a hint of truth to it). The priest has no regular bread, only the bread of the Presence: twelve loaves of pure wheat flour set before God each Sabbath in gratitude for his daily provision for Israel. This the priest gives to David.

David asks for counsel, and Ahimelech inquires of the Lord for him by casting sacred lots.

Lastly, David asks for a weapon, and the priest replies, "The sword of Goliath the Philistine, whom you killed in the Valley of Elah, is here; it is wrapped in a cloth behind the ephod. If you want it, take it; there is no sword here but that one."

"There is none like it; give it to me," David says (1 Sam. 21:9), and the priest does.

Now what David has is not just bread, but bread consecrated to God.

Not just direction, but direction from the sacred lots of God.

Not just a sword, but the sword of Goliath, sanctified by God.

Most Bible scholars would say David's destiny was made known the day the prophet Samuel anointed his head with oil, in a private ceremony with his brothers and father, as God's choice for Israel's next king. But I wonder if he was really given his assignment on this day.

All his natural abilities and duties—as a food bearer, as a brave shepherd boy certain of his call to defend the name of God, as a warrior—were consecrated, made holy, for the work ahead.

And when David does become king, after Saul is no longer alive to vex him, he is responsible for fighting the battles that secure the promised land, completing the task Joshua had started, who was completing the task Moses had started.

David asks God if he can build him a temple, but God tells him no, because he is a man of war. Building the temple is not his assigned task, but his son's.

David's task is to be a warrior-king, and for that to happen, his slingshot has to be replaced by a sword.

There is none like Goliath's, after God got ahold of it.

JESUS' GIFT

How Mary felt the day her soul was pierced by a different kind of sword is not how she would feel two days later. I think that's what Father John was driving at, during Matthew's funeral, when he said that sometimes God's will for a son is to break his mother's heart. The wound is not meant to be permanent. "God's hard words are never his last words," F. B. Meyer wrote. "The woe and the waste and the tears of life belong to the interlude and not to the finale."[6]

The finale is not an event or a point in time but a place. The finale is heaven. Because sometimes God's will for a son is to open the gates of heaven.

By his death and resurrection, Jesus was providing a home for not only Mary but for all those who follow his call, who accept their divinely appointed tasks. What he asked of John was for the time being: Jesus went to prepare a permanent, eternal home for Mary—and for us—in heaven. All other gifts of passage give us a hint of heaven, but only Jesus' gift *is* heaven.

His dying gift is eternal life in an eternal place where death is conquered. But until then, there are gifts that offer what we need to carry on, until *we* get there, to be reunited with the gift givers.

Jean's son, Matthew, had told his friends on the playground at recess the Friday before his death, the last day of school before spring break, that he was going to die soon. He told them they should not worry; he would send the angels down to comfort them. (Jesus had also promised a Comforter before he went to heaven.) When Matthew's friends—his inner circle—returned to school the Monday after spring break and found he had been killed, they confided in their parents his last words of comfort.

That Matthew may have known he was going to die and was not afraid but concerned for his friends meant a lot to Jean; it was a balm to counter the sword piercing through.

Blessed are those who mourn, Jesus said, but he didn't stop there. He gave the reason the mournful are blessed: for they shall be comforted.

Jean *was* comforted by Matthew's parting words. That's why she was able to kick us up from the floor of the lake, to keep us from drowning. It was the gift she needed to carry on.

And it was not the first time Jesus chose to honor a mother by providing for her care.

Chapter 8

LEAPS OF FAITH

Oh, he flies through the air with the greatest of ease
The daring young man on the flying trapeze.

—GEORGE LEYBOURNE,
"THE MAN ON THE FLYING TRAPEZE"

KELLY DILLON WAS my best friend when I was six. I have a snapshot of the two of us resting on a bench, taking a short break from the activity offered by our local amusement park, Fantasy Farm (which for years I pronounced Fancy Farm). There was nothing fancy about it, but it did have lots of rides and a petting zoo, which is why they could call it a farm. In the photo my short brown hair is sweaty and stuck to my head, and I'm smiling broadly; Kelly is beside me, her long blonde hair unmussed under a sailor hat, framing her cool cheek and half smile. She is the picture of poise. Everything about Kelly was poised. Even her dolls were poised. It's not just that her Barbies were always impeccably dressed or even fully clothed (most of mine were scattered naked in our basement), but they were untouched. Literally, not touched.

She didn't play with them because she didn't want them dirtied or mussed up or less than pristine. I have a vague memory of her pulling them out of her bedroom closet for me to look at (did her eyes shift side to side first?), just for a moment, and then quickly returning them to their original boxes. I always marveled at her restraint and wished my naked, strewn dolls were better kept, but hers were a collection, and mine were toys. I sweated at Fancy Farm; her sailor hat never even shifted.

There was only a single ride Kelly consented to during our outing that day. And she had to wait nearly the entire day to ride it, after my sisters and I had exhausted all the more daring rides. It was the merry-go-round. Kelly would only ride on the merry-go-round. Six-year-olds don't dip into the psyches of their friends, so I never found out why. Perhaps it was because it was safe and slow, and you didn't even have to go up and down if you chose a horse that didn't have a movable pole sticking through it. No sudden jerks, no surprise turns, no losing your stomach through your throat. No thrill. Slowly, safely, moving in one direction, with musical accompaniment. A world of adventure awaited—flying cars, a roller coaster, a clown swing—but Kelly chose the merry-go-round.

Poet laureate Mark Strand, in his poem "2032," personifies death as an old man in a limousine waiting for his driver. Figuratively defanged and declawed (or at least unscythed), the grim reaper sits as an old man with a blanket spread across his thighs, wondering, *Where is my driver?* As images go, he is about as menacing as a merry-go-round.

Perhaps death *has* lost its teeth, become more domesticated than it used to be, before the advances in medicine or the birth of the antiaging industry. People want more control over how and when they or their loved ones die, in attempts to prolong the inevitable. But death—real death, and not the one with a blanket across its lap—has a sense of poetic timing not to be tinkered with.

How else to explain the fact that Thomas Jefferson and John Adams, both U.S. presidents and Founding Fathers, died within hours of each other on the Fourth of July, exactly fifty years to the day after the Declaration of Independence was adopted? When fellow Founding Father (and the president sandwiched between the two) James Madison was given the option to falsely extend his life so that he could die on the Fourth of July like his friends (James Monroe had also died on Independence Day five years before), he refused to take it. Death, he was convinced, has its own timing. He died without fanfare on June 27, having allowed the grim reaper his place in the driver's seat.[1]

Of course, if the days of a person's life are allotted by God, as Job and the psalmist David attest (Job 14:5; Ps. 139:16), then death can only figuratively ever be in the driver's seat. Still, I wonder if death's timing is an important factor in understanding gifts of passage. Is it possible that at times death (as the second agent) *chooses* the gift of passage with its sense of timing? In a high-stakes game of "made you look," it points back to the last thing the person did or said, making us take notice.

To flesh out this idea, I turn for help to a friend of a friend, on a similar path. If my journey to understand death began at a mountain cabin in the woods, then his began at a place more like Fantasy Farm.

The image of a merry-go-round was too safe for him, the image of a doddering old man too weak. Instead, the image he chose to help him come to terms with death had both thrills and teeth.

It was a flying trapeze.

The last time I saw Fred Rogers in person, I was sitting in the back of his studio while he taped an episode of *Mister Rogers' Neighborhood*. During a break, he called to me from the set, across the darkened hollow that separated us, asking if I had ever read the works of spiritual writer Henri Nouwen. Henri was a good friend of Fred's, and Fred had just been to Henri's funeral. This was not the first time Fred had asked me to read Henri's work, and I felt a twinge of guilt when I again responded that I had not. "You would just love him," he called back.

I didn't start reading Henri's books until after Fred died (both to honor him and to assuage the guilt) and in earnest after my dad's death. I think Fred knew what he was doing back then, taking the red thread that bound him to Henri and making room in it for me. Henri and I were parallel friends whose paths never intersected: "I am not the rose, but I have lived near the rose," Benjamin Constant wrote.[2] "Living near" meant the fragrance of his friendship with Fred sometimes mingled with my own. In the diary of his final year, Henri wrote about things regarding Fred that affected us both, events that I myself have written about. So I felt connected to a man I had never met or talked to, a rose the only degree of separation between us.

Henri, it turned out, was not only a parallel friend; he was also on a parallel path. I wanted to understand dying gifts; he wanted to understand death.

That's where the flying trapeze came in.

To understand why a circus act was important to Henri, I needed to get to know him better. I already knew some things about him from Fred, and from others I gleaned even more: Noted for his vulnerability as a writer, Henri had a great capacity for attachment, with an "inner circle" of nearly fifteen hundred personal friends (six hundred of whom are mentioned by name in one of his yearlong diaries). A Holland-born Catholic priest who studied psychology, he had a prestigious teaching career that included stints at Notre Dame, Yale, and Harvard. Eventually giving up his post at the latter to live among the disabled at the L'Arche Daybreak community in Toronto, he personally cared for a severely disabled man named Adam. College classes are taught about him, his forty books are widely read and translated, and of his stature as a spiritual writer, *America Magazine* proclaimed: "Only Thomas Merton and C. S. Lewis have had a comparable impact on Christian spirituality in the United States."[3]

All important and impressive things to know about Henri, but none gives me an inkling as to why he chose a flying trapeze as his guiding image, as the passageway to eternity. Hooded creatures, a candle blown out, waning moons—all common images for death. But Henri's chosen specter was circus equipment, with its own theme song.

> *Oh, he flies through the air with the greatest of ease*
> *The daring young man on the flying trapeze,*
> *His movements are graceful; all girls he does please*
> *And my love he has purloined away.*[4]

But Henri instinctively saw beyond the "one-man show" aspect of the trapeze, the misperception that made the girls in this song swoon. What Henri saw was a relationship, a unique dynamic between the man who flies through the air with the greatest of ease and the partner who catches him.

Henri was with his father in Freiburg in 1991 when he first saw the Flying Rodleighs, trapeze artists performing in the German Circus Siemoneit-Barum. "I will never forget how enraptured I became when I first saw the Rodleighs move through the air," he wrote, "flying and catching as elegant dancers."[5] So enraptured was he that he attended the circus again the next day and introduced himself to the trapeze artists, and their instant friendship resulted in more shows, dinners together, and eventually, Henri's touring with the troupe.

"It is hard to describe," he wrote of seeing the Rodleighs for the first time, "but it is the emotion coming from the experience of an *enfleshed spirituality*. Body and spirit are fully united. The body in its beauty and elegance expresses the spirit of love, friendship, family, and community, and the spirit never leaves the here and now of the body."[6]

But at some point the spirit does leave the here and now of the body, and as his knowledge of the trapeze increased, so did Henri's understanding of its meaning.

One day while talking to Rodleigh, the leader of the troupe, Henri asked about the inner workings of the act. What was the secret to his spectacular long jump?

Rodleigh was quick to explain that the flyer is not the great star of the show—contrary to the impression left by the famous song—but the real star is Joe, his catcher.

"The secret," Rodleigh told him, "is that the flyer does nothing and the catcher does everything. When I fly to Joe, I have simply to stretch out my arms and hands and wait for him to catch me and pull me safely over the apron behind the catch bar."[7] It is the catcher's split-second precision, snatching the flyer from the air, that deserves the roar of applause.

Henri was in disbelief: "You do nothing?"

"The worst thing the flyer can do is to try to catch the catcher. I am not supposed to catch Joe. It's Joe's task to catch me."

If he tried to grab Joe's wrists, Rodleigh explained, he might break them or Joe might break his. There is only one way it works: "A flyer must fly, and a catcher must catch, and the flyer must trust, with outstretched arms, that his catcher will be there for him."

Then Henri saw it clearly: dying is trusting in the Catcher.

THE DARING YOUNG MAN

The flying trapeze serves as a central image for another writer, the young hero of the William Saroyan short story "The Daring Young Man on the Flying Trapeze," published in 1934. The story, about a young writer struggling to find work during the Depression, follows the protagonist through a single day. The young man, in his early twenties, is not after his big break; he is only trying to find work to survive, but even a typing job eludes him. There is no work, and without work, no money: "Every meal was bread and coffee and cigarettes, and now he had no more bread. Coffee without bread could never honestly serve as supper, and there were no weeds in the park that could be cooked as spinach is cooked."[8] Yet he is certain he will live to see another day, his confidence bolstered by the fact that the next day's rent has already been paid. Walking the streets in search of work, his mind hums the lyrics to a popular tune:

He flies through the air with the greatest of ease.

Before he finishes the verse, his thoughts break in: "Amusing it was, astoundingly funny. A trapeze to God, or to nothing, a flying trapeze to some sort of eternity." He moves from one arid interview to the next, finding a penny in the gutter along the way, and then seeks refuge at the YMCA, where he has access to paper and ink to write. He works for an hour on a new piece he is writing, then returns to his room, but his energy to write—on the stolen paper from the Y—has left him. He feels nauseated, as if coming apart. His last thought is that he should at least give the penny he found that morning to a child, as "a child could buy any number of things with a penny."

But before he can, the young writer "swiftly, neatly, with the grace of a young man on the trapeze" dies, facedown on the bed that has been rented for another day.

Swan Songs

Perhaps the young man's half-written story is his swan song, like the achingly beautiful melody a swan trills just once in its lifetime, in the moments before it dies. But I think the lone penny holds more meaning; it stands as a symbol of a selfless final thought under the worst possible circumstances. No matter that the act itself is never fulfilled; sometimes the desire is enough.

"Death sets a thing significant," Emily Dickinson observed, "the eye had hurried by."[9] Death makes us take notice of last things, even simple things like pennies. Joan Didion lamented the fact that she carelessly closed the dictionary her husband had been using before he died without noticing the word he was looking up. That it was the last word—in his world of words—he sought out made it significant to her, infused it with new meaning. She had lost something when she closed the dictionary.

So as not to lose something, we slow our eye to honor death's timing; it has, after all, the split-second precision of the Catcher.

———

When Charles Schulz was diagnosed with colon cancer after suffering a stroke in November 1999, he made the painful decision to give up his comic strip, *Peanuts*, which had run in newspapers for nearly fifty years. Charlie Brown, the blockheaded everyman of the funny papers, was a reflection of the man who inked him, shy and hapless and never able to win the love of the little red-haired girl (the real-life red-haired girl was a woman who had rejected Charles Schulz's marriage proposal).

Schulz had hoped to be drawing the strip well into his eighties, but at age seventy-seven, he was through. Cancer had forced his hand, literally, and it pained him that he wasn't able to make the decision on his own.

Because his last original strip was scheduled to run two months after he announced his retirement, the world took the opportunity to honor Charles Schulz in the meantime. Tributes poured forth in newspapers, and Charles, known to his friends as Sparky, was able to read them all and even watch a television special honoring his work. The special, which aired two days before the final strip ran, was hosted by Walter Cronkite, the most trusted man in America. It was as if Sparky was being given the chance to listen in on his own eulogy.

But the greater honor came with death's sense of poetic timing. Charles Schulz died in his sleep of a heart attack at his California home the night before the last strip ran, and just hours before the Sunday papers were delivered to their doorsteps on the opposite coast.

Charles had had a clause in his contract stipulating that the strip would end with his death. What it meant, of course, was that the *Peanuts* characters would never be passed along—like Elijah's mantle—to a successor. But death infused a straightforward legal clause with new meaning.

Charles had once said, "Why do musicians compose symphonies and poets write poems? They do it because life wouldn't have any meaning for them if they didn't. That's why I draw cartoons. It's my life."[10]

When one ended, so did the other.

Charles might not have been able to choose when his career would end, but death had chosen his parting gift with its timing. With Snoopy at the typewriter, a note of gratitude to readers, and a montage of his beloved characters, death had set significant his farewell message.

It had used Charles's own words, his own artistry, to honor his passing.

It made his last strip his epitaph.

WITH BOUNDLESS CONFIDENCE

In the fall of 1995, Henri Nouwen embarked on what he called his sabbatical journey, a year of rest dedicated to writing, praying, and solitude. He kept a detailed diary of his efforts, just as I have during my time of searching for dying gifts, and filled up seven hundred pages with his daily notes. As the year ended, he felt ready for a new direction.

Henri began his sabbatical by reciting a prayer written by Charles de Foucauld, a nineteenth-century aristocrat whose conversion led him into a solitary life as a servant to the poor. Known as the Prayer of Abandonment, from a writer who knew what that meant, it begins, "Father, I abandon myself into your hands." The prayer ends with this stirring surrender:

> Into your hands I commend my spirit.
> I offer it to you with all the love that is in my heart.
> For I love you, Lord, and so want to give myself,
> To surrender myself into your hands,
> Without reserve and with boundless confidence,
> For you are my Father.[11]

Henri prayed the prayer of abandonment every day after that, and it took on special significance on Good Friday, as it echoed the words Jesus spoke from the cross. Henri returned to the L'Arche community to officiate the service, and as he did every Good Friday, he recited the words for the veneration of the cross:

"Behold, behold, the wood of the cross on which is hung our salvation," said Henri.

"Oh, come, let us adore," responded the people.

But in this case, the cross being venerated had no wood, at least not when it was given to Henri.

Four years earlier Henri had met an old Franciscan priest in Freiburg—the same place he met the Flying Rodleighs—while the priest was dying of cancer. He wanted Henri to have a gift before he died, a crucifix with a unique history. The priest had traveled to Croatia with a group of young Germans to restore a church that had been destroyed during the Second World War. A crucifix had been found in the rubble, and the Croatian pastor, recognizing the Germans' ministry of reconciliation, gave it to them as a gift. Now it was being given to Henri as a gift of passage from the old dying priest.

When the crucifix had been unearthed in the rubble, the carved body of Jesus had been torn from the cross beams. The cross beams had been lost or destroyed, and all that was left was the broken body of Christ—hands outstretched, feet nailed together—suspended in air.

"Into your hands I commend my spirit," said Jesus—the one true enfleshed spirituality—trusting too.

"Without reserve and with boundless confidence," prayed Henri—and was caught midair.

A Trophy Life

Symbols are important not because of what they are but because of what they represent: a gold ring, a red fern or thread, wooden beams that intersect to form a cross or attach to rope to form a trapeze. Gifts of passage are important because of what they represent too; they are tangible things that give body to the intangible.

That's what I was thinking the day I opened the newspaper and read about the softball trophy.

The story was about Al Marsh, a local sports store owner who was being honored for his life's work.[12] The honor was bestowed upon him not simply for running a sports store for forty years (or for being the first to open one), but for the kindness he showed: helping out when parents couldn't afford baseball equipment for their children; giving bats, balls, and gloves to teams that needed them on a pay-as-you-go basis; being ready with a key—he lived right next to the store—for off-hour needs. Al even built a base-ball field behind the store for kids to play on.

Local admirers worked a decade to get Softball Hall of Fame recognition for Al. When they finally succeeded, 250 people packed the banquet hall, most of whom had traveled from out of town or state to honor the man who had sold them their first glove or sponsored their first softball team.

Moments before his acceptance speech, Al turned to his friend Leroy, the coach of one of his teams, with this offering: he wanted Leroy to have a softball trophy that was kept at the store. Leroy found the timing odd, the gift unusual. It was a symbol of their shared victory—why give it away now, when it meant the most to him? He wasn't able to get an answer to his question because it was time for Al to give his acceptance speech.

"I'll remember this for the rest of my life," Al said as he fin-ished his remarks, never guessing the rest of his life could be measured in minutes. Then, after thanking his wife, he fell to the floor.

Al, who had no history of heart trouble, was rushed to a hos-pital where he died of heart failure, just like Charles Schulz. Their shared cause of death wasn't the only similarity; they were both seventy-seven years old and died just as their lifelong achieve-ments were being recognized.

But there was something even more significant. The Sunday before he died, Al had attended a church service and prayed, for the first time in his life, a prayer of abandonment (just as Henri had done). He had asked for forgiveness from his sins, surrendering himself—without reserve and with boundless confidence—into the hands of the Father. He wanted a place in heaven.

Al's last gesture of generosity as he was being honored turned out to be his dying gift, and a symbol too. It was a trophy that represented not only a victory on earth but one in heaven. He had been caught by the Catcher—and just in time.

A LESS PERFECT SERMON

Several years ago I dreamed I was inside a large house, so large that a hot-air balloon fit easily inside. Standing on balconies were people, my husband and children among them, who had been invited to ride in the hot-air balloon, which rested on the floor of a large ballroom. The entire event seemed perfectly safe; there was plenty of room, and the balloon could only move straight up and down. Still, as I waited in line, I felt fearful.

Due to some sort of mix-up, I didn't get my turn, although everyone else did, and I was sent on a wild-goose chase around the house. At one point I found myself in a grand foyer, and I stepped outside the front door. Coming toward me on the front steps was a hot-air balloon, with my ten-year-old daughter, Emily, alone in its basket. A group of children was underfoot, guiding her as she landed right in front of me. I was shocked to know what she had been doing, relieved that she was okay, and then angry that she had undertaken such a dangerous task without permission. How was she able to land safely? The children had guided her, she told me. I was still upset, but my shock slowly gave way to chagrin as I realized what had happened. While I was calculating a much lesser risk inside, my daughter had chosen the right atmosphere for flight—a limitless sky, free of restraints, free of control, full of risk and reward.

Her spirit had chosen to fly.

And my spirit? It had donned a sailor hat and waited all day in the hot sun for a chance to ride the merry-go-round.

I think Henri felt that way too. He realized during his sabbatical year that he had been going around in the same circle, meeting the same expectations, saying the same things, humming the same tune. Choosing the lesser risk. He was ready for the trapeze, but he wasn't sure those around him were.

"For me many new questions and concerns emerge," he wrote in his diary, "that weren't there in the past. They refer to all the levels of life: community, prayer, friendship, intimacy, work, church, God, life, and death. How can I be free enough and let the questions emerge without fearing the consequences? I know I am not yet completely free because the fear is still there."[13]

He once told a minister friend that he thought the friend would fare better in the pulpit if he tried to preach a "less perfect sermon," that spontaneity and offering himself more vulnerably "might touch hearts more deeply."

That's what Henri had decided in his sabbatical year, to offer himself as a less perfect sermon. The man noted for his vulnerability was ready to peel off another layer. And it was all deeply and mysteriously tied to his epiphany of the trapeze:

"There in the air I saw the artistic realization of my deepest yearnings. It was so intense that even today I do not dare to write about it because it requires a radical new step not only in my writing but also in my life."

Suddenly the trapeze became not only an image of death but a directive on how to live. Jump and trust, fly spiritually—write in new ways, love in new ways, be more vulnerable, strive for *enfleshed spirituality.* Commending your spirit is not a final prayer of death; it is a daily act of abandonment.

Then Henri saw it clearly: *living* is trusting in the Catcher.

THE DRESS REHEARSAL

In July of 1996, Henri got a chance to try out the trapeze, the real trapeze, for the first time. He was visiting the Flying Rodleighs again and had planned to write a book about them when he returned from his sabbatical, which was nearing its end. After a practice session, Rodleigh asked if he'd like to try to be the flyer. "It is an intimidating place to be," he wrote of the climb up the long ladder to the pedestal. "The space below, above, and around me felt enormous and awesome."[14] With a safety belt around him and a net below, Henri grabbed onto the bar and swung a few times, kicking like a child on a swing to get greater height. Out of breath, he dropped into the net and began the series again, "with a tiny bit more grace." Then, in order to give himself a sense of not only flying but being caught, he climbed the ladder to the catcher's side, and the catcher, hanging upside down on the bar, dangled Henri by his wrists. Watching the video of the practice session, including his stint as the daring young man, made Henri feel very silly, but he conceded, "It got me as close as I will ever come to being a trapeze artist!" Armed with the literal experience, Henri was ready for its spiritual counterpart. It was time for new direction in his life and ministry, time for his long jump, his foray into what he called his new consciousness, time to take the risk.

He had had the dress rehearsal; he was ready to start living.

HENRI'S GIFT

Henri had always planned to publish his sabbatical journal in book form, but it was never supposed to bear the subtitle it was eventually given: *The Diary of His Final Year*. He died unexpectedly of a massive heart attack three weeks after making the last entry.

No one (on earth) knows why Henri didn't get his chance to fly. Sometimes, as with the young Depression-era writer, a penny is left ungiven. Or the gift that is left is imperfect or incomplete, like the war-torn crucifix. Sometimes the gift that is left is a desire, and that is enough.

A desire—with a symbol. A penny, a word in the dictionary, a comic strip, a softball trophy. And one thing more.

When Henri left behind a diary that preserved the thoughts and emotions of his final year, he also left with it his gift of passage, a symbol that gave body to his greatest desire, a gift that honored his bravest intent.

Along with his carefully articulated desire to fly spiritually and his unflinching trust in the Catcher, Henri left behind his understanding that turning a corner sometimes means you have to stop turning in circles and take a leap. And for that, you need a trapeze.

GIFTS *of*
INTRIGUE

Chapter 9

WHEN SORROW
NEEDS A MAP

I said to my silent, curious Soul, out of the bed of the slumber-chamber, Come, for I have found the clue I sought so long.

—WALT WHITMAN, *Leaves of Grass*

"FAMOUS LAST WORDS."

The phrase used to refer to dying quotes, the last words attributed to people of renown (they being the "famous" part), spoken as they drew their last breath. "I shall hear in heaven," Beethoven is reported to have said as he lay dying. Most scholars agree these were most likely not his final words, but through either legend or the initial spin of those closest to him, they continue to be linked to his dying breath.

When John Adams was on his deathbed and was asked if he knew what day it was, he answered, "Oh, yes; it is the glorious Fourth of July. It is a great day. It is a good day. God bless it. God bless you all." Then he lapsed into unconsciousness. Rousing from it momentarily, he uttered two words before breathing his last (and these are verifiable): "Thomas Jefferson." Jefferson, as I've mentioned, had preceded Adams in death by only a few hours, but Adams had not been told that his once political rival turned faithful friend and pen pal had passed away. Perhaps during that sacred window, that brief overlap of heaven and earth, Adams was able to see his friend and called out to him.[1]

That's what "famous last words" used to mean. But when the phrase is used now, the take is comic and satirical as opposed to tragic and profound.

Examples include remarks such as "Is this the wire I'm supposed to cut?" "What's the worst that can happen?" "I wonder where the mother bear is." And almost anything uttered by a teenager in a slasher movie.

Famous last words.

Sometimes they are true-life stories that show a perilous lack of foresight, as when Memphis musician Eddie Bond rejected a young Elvis for his band, telling him to stick with truck driving because he was never going to make it as a singer anyway.

Or the declaration to his congregation of Bishop Milton Wright—father to Orville and Wilbur—that if God had intended man to fly, he would have given him wings.

I uttered famous last words myself last Friday when I told a friend she *had* to read a famous fiction writer's autobiography. "I just love her nonfiction," I gushed, and three days later I found out that there's more conjured-up stuff in her autobiographical works than in her fantasies.

What are the chances that this discovery would come on the heels of my glowing endorsement? The irony and timing make them famous last words.

But last words need not always be the stuff of legends or the brunt of jokes. They don't always have to portend regret.

Sometimes they can leave a clue.

The Soul Selects Her Own Society

Whenever my daughter and I take our daily walks around the neighborhood (where I uncover most of my pennies from heaven), I always point to a stately but strange-looking house atop a hill and say, "That reminds me of Emily Dickinson." I have never been to Emily Dickinson's real home in Massachusetts, and only recently saw a photo of it. But even so, the house reminds me of her: it sits awkwardly on its lot (as though it doesn't quite belong there), is shrouded by trees (as if it's enchanted), and has an air of aloofness about it (punctuated by a steep staircase that leads uninvitingly to its front door).

Besides what Mrs. Harris taught me in high school, all I know about Emily Dickinson is the mystique that surrounds her, a vague impression that makes me link her to forlorn houses in my neighborhood. But now I want to know more. Emily Dickinson has taught me that death sets things significant, and this insight has helped me to understand the nature of dying gifts. Hers is no small contribution, which makes me want to know what *her* death was like, what *thing* it "set significant."

But I'm not ready to know the answers. The red thread has some work to do to bind me to this enigmatic poet. Taking me by the shoulders, it shakes me loose of my preconceptions, makes me walk up the steep staircase of my pretend Emily Dickinson house, and knock on the front door. It's time to find out who is really inside.

The real Emily Dickinson, I soon discover, is complex enough to be a character lifted from the pages of the Gothic novels written by her nineteenth-century contemporaries. I was at least right about her aloofness; she came into the world and departed from it having barely left the site of both events, the brick house in Amherst her family called the Homestead. As an adult, she dressed always in white and offered the rare visitor to her home the choice of a glass of wine or a rose from her well-tended garden.

But it wasn't always that way. The same woman known as the "poet of dread" after her death was also called the Belle of Amherst during a brimming and perfectly normal girlhood. She was not a one-note eccentric but seemed to slide seamlessly back and forth between the extreme ends of any scale. She bared her soul in reams of poetry, and yet doctors trying to diagnose the illness that took her life had to do so through the crease of a partially opened door. She wrote poignantly about death but sat in her bedroom while her father's funeral was conducted on the family lawn outside. She wrote passionately of what Lewis called "that kind of love which lovers are 'in'" but never married. She wrote nearly eighteen hundred poems, and yet only seven were published in her lifetime, five in a local newspaper. None had her name attached. When she died, her newspaper obituary mainly lauded her as a gifted gardener.

She abhorred household duties charged to women, but she found a way to artfully sew together stationery paper to create the booklets that housed her secret poetry.

She was a hermit with a vibrant circle of acquaintances and a deep connection to the outside world, which poured in through correspondence with friends and family and from the influence of the occasional visitor. A popular hermit? Her soul selected her own society, as she wrote in one of her poems, and "then shut the door."

Why she would cloister herself like a nun to write poetry no one was permitted to read or publish is another mystery, another paradox in the life of the Belle of Amherst. She was not out to perfect the form of poetry, as her early letters show her imagination extended to both spelling and grammar, enough to bleed dry the red pen of any middle school English teacher. Instead, she defined poetry purely in terms of its visceral effects: "If I read a book and it makes my whole body so cold no fire can ever warm me, I know *that* is poetry. If I feel physically as if the top of my head were taken off, I know *that* is poetry. These are the only ways I know it. Is there any other way?"[2]

That she was successful in producing that effect herself is evident from the words of friend, pen pal, and literary editor Thomas Wentworth Higginson, who lyrically and aptly described her work as "poetry torn up by the roots, with rain and dew and earth still clinging to them."[3]

In fact, it was Higginson who was responsible, directly or indirectly, for her secret stash of poetry remaining secret. She entrusted to him some of her poems, and while accounts vary, either he attempted to conform her poetry to the style of the day, leaving Emily looking for the nearest exit (figuratively, of course), or else he discouraged her outright from having her work published. It may have been the latter, as he affectionately called Emily his "partially cracked poetess at Amherst."[4]

That she is now considered—along with Walt Whitman, whose quotation opens this chapter—one of the two most innovative voices in nineteenth-century American literature is wondrous, indeed. And the explanation for how that happened, I am about to discover, lies in her famous last words.

In her final words, as in her poetry, there was a hidden riddle. The poetess of obliquity was oblique unto the end. Or was she? Perhaps instead of giving a riddle, she was providing its answer, or instead of devising another labyrinth with her words, she was pointing the way through it—to the trove that lay at its center.

Emily Dickinson was leaving a clue.

SORROW'S MAP

C. S. Lewis was foraging his house again after Joy's death, looking for a used notebook that would offer up a few blank pages. He was fortunate this time, as the notebook was bare except for a few scribbles of arithmetic toward the back. It was the fourth and last notebook he would fill with thoughts eventually comprising *A Grief Observed*, as he resolved not to buy any new books for the purpose of indulging his grief. In addition, he found that one of his motivations for doing so had been based on a misunderstanding:

> I thought I could describe a *state*; make a map of sorrow. Sorrow, however, turns out to be not a state but a process. It needs not a map but a history, and if I don't stop writing that history at some quite arbitrary point, there's no reason why I should ever stop. There is something new to be chronicled every day.[5]

But sometimes sorrow does need a map, and the dying person provides the clue to finding it.

Deciphering such clues has been the lifework of hospice nurses and authors Maggie Callanan and Patricia Kelley, whose concept of "nearing death awareness" has encouraged loved ones to look for significance in what the dying say and do. Callanan and Kelley see what was once dismissed as confusion or hallucinations as special communication from the dying, which in many cases describes what the dying person is experiencing or what he or she needs for a peaceful death. Their advice is not to dismiss, but to pay attention.

One of the experiences from their decade-long work with the dying involves a young man in his late twenties, a high school football coach diagnosed with cancer, initially overcome only to resurface in other parts of his body.[6] (Cancer, my father's oncologist had told us, is never cured. It is only maintained.)

The football coach had moved back in with his parents, who provided his care, and while he was weak, he was expected to live for several months. One Saturday evening, the father noticed a change in his son, something he couldn't put his finger on. He called the hospice nurse to tell her something was "different." When the hospice nurse arrived, she could find no physical changes in the young man. Later, talking with his parents, she was shown a piece of paper their son had been working on that day.

On the paper was the diagram of a football play. The parents could easily have overlooked a scrap of paper with a scribbled football play; after all, their son was a football coach and his siblings were to join him the next afternoon to watch a football game together. It could have been a mindless doodle or wishful thinking for the next day's game.

But the hospice nurse, wondering if it was a clue, took a closer look. Two teams had been drawn on the diagram. The players on one team were marked with the initials of the young football coach, his parents, and his siblings. An arrow had been drawn from the young man's circle out of bounds, with the words "Out of the game by noon on Sunday."

The hospice nurse encouraged the parents not to be dismissive. The siblings who had intended to come over Sunday afternoon to watch a football game were asked to come in the morning instead.

The next day the young man visited with each member of his family, and then, just before noon, he became restless, asking his mother to rearrange his pillows. He lay back down on the straightened pillows and died.

An autopsy revealed that his death was not directly related to the cancer; a blood clot in his lungs was responsible, a condition the dying man could not have known about.

The scribbled football play, with its words and familiar symbols, provided a map of sorrow for the family. It pointed toward the time of the young man's death and gave each family member an opportunity to say good-bye.

They were glad they had paid attention.

———

While sorting through her husband's office files after his death, Donna, who lived for many years in my hometown, found an unpublished short story she didn't know her husband had written.[7] Composed two years earlier, it tells the story of a newly widowed woman he named Emily (perhaps a nod to his favorite poet). Emily is a church organist, trying to make it through her first

Christmas without her husband. She composes a piece for him, which she plays in his honor in a special Christmas performance.

As she read the short story, Donna, herself a church organist, was coping with the death of her husband, a retired newspaperman. She was not asked to play the organ on Christmas but on Palm Sunday, a month after her husband had died of an aneurysm. Playing the organ so soon after his death, Donna felt just like her fictional counterpart, who concludes the short story with the prayer that somehow her husband is hearing her play.

Perhaps he was, and Beethoven too.

The prescience of Donna's husband was shown in other ways: He had recently moved them to a smaller house requiring no yard work, across the street from the church where Donna played the organ. All practical steps to prepare her for being alone. But what about the nonpractical elements? What about her grief? For that he left her a short story in a place he knew she would find it—a map of sorrow to navigate through her pain and come out on the other side.

Which she did, just like Emily.

———

Martin Toler Jr. was the only miner with an ink pen.

Miners don't usually carry pens into the mine with them; there's no need for a pen unless you're the section foreman, which Martin was. With dim light and limited oxygen, he turned over an insurance form he had found in his pockets, scavenging for blank space as C. S. Lewis had done. He scratched the pen on the paper to get the ink flowing and wrote:

Tell all I'll see them on the other side.
It wasn't bad
Just went to sleep.
I love you.

Martin Toler was one of thirteen miners trapped after an explosion ripped through the Sago coal mine in West Virginia on January 2, 2006, during the first shift of the new year. Martin, who was fifty-one, had spent more than half his life in the mines. His family members, and those of the other twelve trapped miners, waited at a church for word and were initially elated when they heard the miners had been found alive. The families' joy turned to incomprehensible grief three hours later when they discovered only one miner had survived.

Martin's nephew said the note, found with his uncle's body, "was the most precious thing that I believe I've ever seen."[8]

Four other notes were recovered by medical examiners, with similar messages of comfort, indications to family that the other miners had just fallen asleep. Martin had shared his ink pen. But that wasn't all. The sole survivor, the only witness to the deaths, later reported that Martin had also shared his faith, leading the miners in a collective prayer for individual forgiveness.

The night before the explosion, Martin had attended church, where the evening's service focused on this passage from Paul's letter to the Colossians: "Set your affection on things above, not on things on the earth" (3:2 KJV).

Things above.

"Tell all I'll see them on the other side."

Martin's "map" was different from those of the young football coach and the retired newspaperman. It didn't show when he was going to die or how his wife would get through the grief. Instead, it pointed to where he was going—and where his crew could be found.

EMILY'S GIFT

Emily Dickinson left a clue, too, in her famous last words. Symptoms of kidney disease began to plague her at age fifty-five, and within a year she was near death. After a few days of semi-consciousness, she whispered four words: "The fog is rising."

And then she died.

Later, her younger sister Lavinia, who likewise never married and lived her entire life with Emily at the Homestead, was riffling through her sister's things in search of her letters, having promised Emily that she would burn them after her death. During the search, Lavinia uncovered something she hadn't expected to find, locked away in the maid's trunk: forty booklets of stationery paper carefully stitched together and holding eight hundred of her sister's poems. Among the completed poems was one Emily had written twenty-five years before. Now known by its title, "I've Seen a Dying Eye,"[9] the poem describes a dying person's last moments, when his eye roves the room as if in search of something, and then:

> . . . *cloudier become;*
> *And then obscure with fog.*

The fog closes the eye of the dying person before he reveals what he sees, what assurance he sought. It's a mystery to the poet watching, waiting, paying attention.

But Emily leaves no such mystery when the fog rises in her own eye. She issues an invitation to search for the origin of her cryptic, dying words. Her words are a map, leading to her undiscovered poetry, the trove deep in the heart of the labyrinth.

She had asked that her letters be burned, but had bid—by her famous last words—that her poems be found. In the end, nearly eighteen hundred of them were unearthed, sewn into booklets, written on scraps of paper and discarded grocery lists. Emily, too, had scavenged for blank spaces.

Lavinia, who knew her sister best, was astounded. Lavinia had never complained about doing the bulk of the housework; she understood that Emily's job was "to think." She just never imagined how much.

Nor had I. My preconceptions about Emily needed to be shaken. She wasn't a starry-eyed dreamer who didn't quite belong; she was a woman with a gift that could have been left ungiven, a poet with a depth and clarity I wouldn't have access to if not for her clue. It was a line from her own poetry, and it led to her gift: hundreds of poems to rouse the sleeping soul. Sometimes the grieving soul, like mine, needs to be roused, too, to find the clue that leads to a dying gift.

In an ending befitting a Gothic novel, Emily Dickinson's coffin—as white as her perennial apparel—went down into the ground. And just as quickly her poems sprang up, with the rain and dew and earth still clinging to them.

She was a gifted gardener, indeed.

Chapter 10

IF ONLY FOR AN HOUR

There are years that ask questions and years that answer.

—ZORA NEALE HURSTON

THE STORY MUST have been written in the fifties, because little girls still wore party dresses. One of the schoolboys is having a birthday party and invites his classmates, who look to be in second grade (the same grade I was in when I read the story). The parents of one of the little girls in the class buy her a brand-new party dress for the occasion. Her friend, once she learns the good news, wants a new party dress too. She begs her parents, who try their best to reason with her, explaining that they cannot afford a new dress. Reason has no color, but envy does, because it's stronger. The little girl mopes around until the day of the party, when she reluctantly allows her old dress to be slipped over her head and buttoned up the back. (The man in the iron mask couldn't have felt more constricted.)

The Norman Rockwell–like illustrations show what happens

next. The party is an active one, as the host is a boy, and we see the little girl in the old dress running around, pinning the tail on the donkey, bobbing for apples, playing musical chairs. She seems to have momentarily forgotten her constriction. At some point she notices her friend is missing and begins looking for her. She finds her sitting on a little chair in the corner, resplendent and alone, unable to enter the party festivities for fear of ruining her new dress.

There are all kinds of things an eight-year-old can take away from a story like that, and perhaps the intent, given the parochial school setting in which it was delivered, was to be content with what you have.

But the story has stuck with me for many years for a different reason, marked as the first time I realized there is a providence to bad news, a fate to disappointment. In the larger scheme of things, an unseen hand moves you toward disappointment because, at the time, it's best for you. At some point you get to know why, but only if you put on the old dress and attend the party. In the meantime, something is withheld from you, and you feel slighted, left out. Why can't you have what someone else gets to have? There are times when this question is especially appropriate.

As when you are committed to a life of celibacy and solitude . . . and you've just fallen in love.

FATED DISAPPOINTMENTS

I wasn't the one committed to a life of celibacy and solitude, but I seriously considered it around the same time I read about the new party dress. I grew up surrounded by clergy, priests who were family friends and nuns who taught me through the eighth grade. Their commitment to God always amazed me, as they gave up the prospect of marriage, of being fathers and mothers. I wanted to be committed to God, too, but I wasn't sure I was cut from the right cloth to wear theirs. So in third grade I asked my parents to buy me a Baby Tender Love, the most realistic doll on the market. If any doll could draw out my maternal instincts, it was Baby Tender Love. I vowed that if I saw a vestige of motherly love surface, I would resign myself to life outside the convent. The results were inconclusive, though, as I insisted on administering the sacraments along with formula to the lifelike doll. (I never could get the Ash Wednesday smudge off her forehead.)

There was a romanticism to a life apart. I can still remember standing around the foursquare court at recess when Sister Evelyn confessed to us that she had been engaged before becoming a nun. I still remember the name of her handsome young fiancé, Tony. She broke off the engagement to become married to God, despite Tony's pleas of undying love. I was still clinging to my Baby Tender Love.

Perhaps I felt a tinge of guilt about this, because when as an adult I discovered that Thomas Merton fell in love (seeking romanticism apart from his life apart), I felt slightly vindicated; after all, his vows of chastity, poverty, and obedience were the same as Sister Evelyn's.

To say that Thomas Merton is one of the greatest spiritual thinkers of the twentieth century is not an idle claim, given that news of his death in 1968 warranted the front page of the *New York Times*. An accidental electrocution during a trip to Asia ended the life of the prolific Trappist monk, whose writings and lectures continue to influence millions with their contemplative spirituality.

I found Thomas Merton through the promptings of another Thomas, the contemporary writer Thomas Moore. His work exposed me to Merton's insights, spoon-feeding me bits and pieces until I was ready to digest him on my own. When I really like what people have to say, and they really like what someone else has to say, then I try to follow the direction of their nod. Fred loved Henri, and now I love Henri (just as he predicted). It's the red thread of recommendation, and it binds just as tightly. Often one recommendation leads to another, and in the end I find that there are links between the individuals that I didn't know existed, as if I've unearthed some secret fraternal order. Sometimes the individuals (recommendations that are two and three times removed from each other) end up being bound by a mutual admiration of or friendship with one another so that the red thread crosses over and weaves through other red threads. It's like the tangled yarn of a child's game that reveals, after many twists and loops, an intended pattern—a cup and saucer or a cat's cradle. That's how I became bound to Thomas Merton.

Merton's life was not an easy one. It was filled with sorrow and (as Helen Keller once noted about the world in general) the overcoming of it. Born in France, he lost his mother when he was six and his father when he was sixteen. He fathered a child out of wedlock while studying at Cambridge University. He relocated to the United States to study at Columbia and became perhaps the first person to experience a religious conversion while writing a master's thesis. His newfound faith was tested when he was locked out of his bid to become a Franciscan monk—the first of many fated disappointments.

Despite these setbacks, the memoir of his conversion, *The Seven Storey Mountain*, published once he had settled into the abbey at Gethsemani in Kentucky as a Trappist monk, became an international best seller. After years in the monastic community at Gethsemani, he fulfilled a long-standing desire to live alone, having been granted permission to live full-time in a hermitage in the woods of Kentucky. His desire for solitude was sometimes thwarted by his international fame, and he was once cynically dubbed "the monk of Times Square." By the time of his death at age fifty-three, he was regarded as one of the most influential clerics of the day, with fifty books and hundreds of poems to his credit. His influence extended beyond spiritual matters to social issues, and his activism in the peace and civil rights movements made him as widely known as his spiritual writings.

Yet not all the sorrows of his life were overcome, and one lay buried in his personal journals, sealed at his request until twenty-five years after his death.

When Gifts Intrigue

Gifts of intrigue are different from other dying gifts because they require an extra measure of vigilance, a closer degree of attention. Sometimes you have to wait patiently for the gift to show itself and come into clear focus. But it's not an active stance, a function of sheer effort (spiritual things never are). It's more like the Magic Eye puzzles, those 3-D illusions that are indiscernible at first glance. You won't see the image if you try too hard; instead, you try to look past it. Once you relax your eye and slowly move away from the background, the image emerges, jumps out at you.

The longer you look, the clearer the image; the farther away you go from it, the deeper it becomes. Time and distance and a relaxed receptivity—the same elements needed to discern gifts of intrigue.

Time was especially a factor in Thomas Merton's gift, because the clue to it, found in his journal, had been hidden for twenty-five years. Except for a summary of what he was going to do that day, the last words Thomas Merton wrote in his journal, which he had kept since a teenager, were these: "Most men will not swim before they are able to."

The words belong to Novalis, a German novelist and poet.

I wondered if these words held special meaning, like the last word Joan Didion's husband looked up in the dictionary, even though the death was unexpected. Somewhere in his heart and mind, did Merton—famed for his inner spirituality, his deep connection to things unseen—know he was going to die? Was he saying he *was* ready to swim; in this case, to enter eternity? Was he in essence saying most men will not die before they are ready?

More has been made of Merton's last spoken words than his written words, as well as the mode of his death, both bracing ironies. His last words were spoken at the end of a lecture delivered at a conference for abbots in Bangkok, Thailand, on December 10, 1968. Since he planned to take questions later, Merton quipped, "And now I will disappear." He literally did, when two hours later his hand touched the faulty switch of an ungrounded electric fan as he left the bath. Others point to the final sentence of his autobiography, which they believe presages the way he died. The book concludes with Merton's transcription of God's assignment for him: "My mercy which has created you for this end . . . that you may become the brother of God and learn to know the Christ of the burnt men."[1]

Of course, Merton was speaking metaphorically, not disguising a death wish. A journal entry explains with trademark poignancy what this image really means:

> I know well the burnt faces of the Prophets and the Evangelists transformed by the white-hot dangerous presence of inspiration, for they looked at God as into a furnace and the Seraphim flew down and purified their lips with fire. I read their books with joy and with "holy fear," and their words became a part of me. They are solemn and dreadful and holy men humbled by the revelation they wrote down. They are my Fathers. They are the "burnt men."[2]

Even a poem he wrote about a fool who falls in love with an electric light ("Do you not know, fool, / That love is dynamite?") is held up as prescient of his death.[3]

But these examples are ironies, not gifts of passage. The gift lies in deciphering the meaning of the last words in his journal, the record of his heart.

Meeting M.

"At 5:30, as I was dreaming in a very quiet hospital, the soft voice of the nurse awoke me gently from my dream—it was like awakening for the first time from all the dreams of my life . . . as if Wisdom had awakened me," Thomas Merton wrote in his journal in 1960, during a brief stay in a hospital.

He continued, writing:

Wisdom cries out in the marketplace—"if anyone is little let him come to me." Who is more little than the helpless man, asleep in bed, having entrusted himself gladly to sleep and to night? Him the gentle voice will awaken, all that is sweet in woman will awaken him. . . . "Woman" . . . Deep is the ocean, boundless sweetness, kindness, humility, silence of wisdom that is *not* abstract, disconnected, fleshless. Awakening us gently when we have exhausted ourselves to night and to sleep."

Six years later, Merton returned to the hospital for back surgery and met another nurse, a young student nurse, who seamlessly stepped into his eloquent personification of wisdom. His fascination with what it is about woman that is not "abstract, disconnected, fleshless" became all at once solidified, connected, and embodied in a young woman he called M.

Astoundingly romantic, except that she is engaged, and he is a monk.

"All monks, as is well known, are unmarried, and hermits more unmarried than the rest of them," Merton himself noted.

At first Merton realized the swift connection was due to her attentiveness as his nurse and the special vulnerability of being cared for. He was almost dismissive of it. Then there was an exchange of letters, followed by declarations of love. These communications led to "illegal" phone calls and clandestine meetings (but no breaking of vows). Folk singer and songwriter Joan Baez, a friend and admirer of Merton, came to visit the hermitage and, moved by Merton's love story, tried to drive him to the hospital where M. was on duty that night. The plan was foiled, and the star-crossed lovers remained momentarily uncrossed.

His poetry from this time (for fear of scandal, it was published only recently) sounds like the ramblings of a besotted teenager. I wrote my very first love poem (the inspiration for which was also named Thomas) in sixth grade, and when it was discovered in my coat pocket by my older sister's boyfriend, I wanted to die. Perhaps the same reasoning went into Merton's twenty-five-year moratorium on his coat pockets.

His romantic notions about the gentle voice that awakens eventually implode; instead, he found himself being awakened in the early morning hours, "in a splendid and terrible crisis of love. . . . I wept for half an hour, shaken with sobs, still not completely awake."

What did wake him was the fact that a fellow monk overheard (or eavesdropped on) a secret phone call to M. and turned him in. (He was caught, of course, because hermits don't have phones, and Merton had to sneak around the monastery to find access to one.)

Two days before he was found out, Merton and M. discussed their future together. Should he forsake his vows? Should he marry her? The questions fell away when their secret love was uncovered, because what was also uncovered was Merton's inability to fight against a society that would deem them outcasts. He decided to keep his vows, almost by default. It is another example of the providence of bad news, another fated disappointment. At the beginning of the relationship, Merton had written that he hoped his fondness for M. didn't turn into an "ugly, bloody" fire. But that's exactly how it ended, when he burned her letters in a pile of pine branches outside his hermitage in the woods—the burnt man burning away his desire for another kind of life.

But later he wondered, had he missed the very point of life?

He began to feel left out again, unable to have what others get to have. And the little girl in her old party dress agrees with him, for now.

YEARS THAT ASK QUESTIONS

Heather and Pete were frustrated, and there was much more at stake than a party dress. They were poised for change, on their way to a new life, and at the last minute, a stumbling block was put in their path.

The first change of plans came courtesy of good fortune, when the home they put on the market sold in eight days. The problem was that their new home, being built by Heather's father, would not be ready by the time the new owners of their old home wanted to move in.

To complicate matters, Heather, a teacher busy finishing up the school year, was six months pregnant with their first child. Heather's parents suggested she and Pete move into their basement for the four to six weeks of final construction. Then they could move into their new home and settle the nest in time for the baby to be born.

That was a manageable disappointment, but the next one was not. The easement on their new property had allowed for right-of-way (a driveway) but had not specified electricity, probably due to the fact that the document dated back to the 1920s. The electrical company wouldn't budge unless they obtained the signatures of all landowners between their home and the road. The process dragged on from weeks to months, with one snag after another. Heather and Pete, my son's youth pastors, enlisted friends, family, and church members to pray for them. Certainly God could move on the hearts of these people to sign off; the hearts of kings were in his hands. But the prayers remained unanswered.

Four weeks in the basement stretched into a year, a year in which their new home sat empty because of a legal snafu. It was such a senseless waste. When Heather and Pete's baby, Jon, was born, his nursery had to be nestled in between the pool table and big-screen TV. Heather felt bad for Joe, her younger brother, a senior in high school, who had made the most use of the basement room and was now exiled from it most of the time.

But there were some hopeful glimmers too. Heather had moved away to college when Joe was only ten, and now she had a chance to get to know him all over again. Her mother had always told her that she and Joe had similar temperaments, but that's not easily discernible when you are eighteen and your brother is ten. Now when Joe sought refuge from teenage angst in the basement, Heather was there to listen. They did have similar temperaments, she soon discovered, and she was able to help him sort through dilemmas she herself had gone through. Her newfound influence as the big sister-confidante was evident in Joe's choice of college when he decided to apply to her alma mater.

Heather, Pete, and Jon moved into their new home as Joe was leaving for college, just as Heather had done when he was ten. Joe had been at his new school in Indiana for only five weeks when he planned to return home for his girlfriend's homecoming. He was en route to Ohio to catch a plane when his car inexplicably swerved left of center and into oncoming traffic, hitting a semi-truck head on. The driver of the truck tried to veer out of Joe's way, but it was too late. Joe had most likely fallen asleep, since a trooper who witnessed the accident never saw Joe's brake lights come on. He died instantly, without suffering or even recognition. There was no evidence that his body had tensed up before the crash, which meant he didn't foresee what was going to happen. He didn't even startle; he just woke up in heaven.

Heather was with a women's group from church on her way to a conference out of state when she got the news. The caravan turned around immediately, but it still took six hours to reach home. During the long drive home, Heather saw the blurred background of a year of frustration fade away and an image begin to emerge.

Joe's dying gift had been wrapped up in unanswered prayer. But God had been anticipating another prayer, answering it before its petition had even formed on Heather's lips.

Heather had been able to share the last year of her brother's life with him, to become reacquainted with him—and he with her. Joe got to know his nephew intimately. The forced exile to the basement had been a year that asked questions.

Now Heather had her answer . . . and her gift.

If Only for an Hour

Soon after Thomas Merton's relationship with the young nurse was found out by his elders, he had a dream about her. In the dream, she was swimming in one of the monastery lakes, alone and dispirited. (It was the second lake dream to have found its way into my year of searching.) Thomas approached the lake, dressed in his frock, the long monk's robe he was required to wear, indicating to her with a wave of his hand that he was coming. She looked as if she didn't believe him. Even if he had to take off his frock and swim naked, he reasoned, he would go to her. As he got closer to the water's edge, he saw one of the abbey's monks there in his way. He could not reach her. She was still in the water, he still on dry ground, when he woke up.

But in reality, and for the rest of his life, the exact opposite would be true of Thomas Merton. He was in the water, where he was supposed to be, because "most men will not swim before they are able to."

I have learned a lot about dying gifts in the year since I began my journey, and I have a strong sense that Thomas's gift lies in these words. But I don't think he was talking about eternity, about being ready to die. The image is deeper than that, so I wait on it, giving it the time and distance it needs.

Then I find a clue: I discover, as the red thread weaves its way through to its intended pattern, that Thomas's last words show up in the work of another solitary writer, Hermann Hesse. In his preface to *Steppenwolf*, Hesse speaks through a young man who has been left his own gift of passage, a manuscript from an erratic and eccentric man named Harry Haller, the "Steppenwolf," or lone wolf, of the title.

In the preface, the young man, the nephew of Steppenwolf's landlady, describes one of his encounters with the enigmatic protagonist. Steppenwolf, who admits that he lives "a bit to one side, on the edge of things," has been reading Novalis and comes upon the same quote that Thomas Merton scratched in his journal just before he died. Steppenwolf is amused and says to the nephew, "Is not that witty? Naturally, they won't swim! They are born for the solid earth, not for the water. And naturally they won't think. They are made for life, not for thought. Yes, and he who thinks, what's more, he who makes thought his business, he may go far in it, but he has bartered the solid earth for the water all the same, and one day he will drown."[4]

The nephew surmises that Steppenwolf had made this barter himself, trading the security of solid ground for the wateriness of the life of contemplation. While Steppenwolf tries to fit in, tries to have what everyone else gets to have, it is, the nephew observes, "as though it were only with an extreme and desperate effort that he could force his way through any crack into our little peaceful world and be at home there, if only for an hour."

I wonder as I read these words if Thomas Merton's relationship with M. was the very thing Steppenwolf was trying for, a touch of the ordinary. Perhaps loving M. gave Thomas a glimpse into what it would have been like had he chosen land and not water as his vocation's home. His way to M. was indeed being blocked, but not by another monk; it was his commitment to making thought his business that stood in the way. M. must have provided the crack into another world, a solid world, and his love for her was his attempt to be at home on land, "if only for an hour."

But the hour was up. To stay in the water, to heed his calling, Thomas Merton needed to be alone. In fact, that's what *monk* means. Alone.

In 2007, poet and author Kathleen Norris was asked to write an introduction to a new book of poetry. The poetry, left unpublished for over three decades, was penned by Thomas Merton and included his love poetry for M. In discussing the relationship between Merton and M., Norton related that the experience was humbling to him and "in the end probably made him a better monk."[5]

A better monk. That was the point. In the end he was still a monk, living a bit to one side, on the edge of things. Given the choice between solid ground and water, Merton chose the water.

While C. S. Lewis's dying gift from Joy sprang from his taking hold of the love between a husband and wife, Merton's gift had to do with letting it go.

"One might say I had decided to marry the silence of the forest," he wrote in his journal.

His dying gift, his last words, point back to the choice he made when he relinquished M.: to continue to enrich the world through his aloneness, his solitary contemplation, the thoughts and prayers that come from a life apart.

In the end, then, Thomas Merton pulled his frock back over his head and attended the party in his old dress. There he discovered that sometimes you feel more left out in a new dress if the old dress is the one you are supposed to be wearing. There is a fate to disappointment.

Sometimes getting what you want can be constricting . . . when your gift is to swim.

A GIFT *from* MY FATHER

Chapter 11

WHAT THE GOOD SON GETS

"My son," the father said, "you are always with me,
and everything I have is yours."

—THE PRODIGAL SON'S FATHER,
TO THE GOOD SON, IN LUKE 15:31

NOW COMES MY own story, pieced together from notes I scratched out during the final days of my dad's life. There was no time to languish on a window seat with pen in hand; instead, words and phrases were scribbled in whatever blank spaces I could find, like Lewis's used arithmetic notebooks and Emily's discarded grocery lists. Most of my words took refuge on the back of my airline itinerary, since I never used the return flight ticket, since I wasn't able to stick to the schedule. The notes sat for a year before I attempted to piece them together in any discernible order, but even then they lacked an ending. I could only tell what had happened, not what any of it meant. Then I went to the mountain cabin; then I spent a year following the red thread. Now I'm ready to know how my story ends.

There are more meaningful things to say when someone is dying, but instead I made a simple request: please tell Elvis I love him, and give Shakespeare a hug for me—and make sure he knows I still read him every year. Eternity hung in the air, but my thoughts were wallowing in the mud with a pompadour and a plume.

Dad would have remembered my three-year love affair with Elvis, which began when I was twelve as I watched *Jailhouse Rock* for the first time on late-night television. His initial amusement over my crush (and relief that a shirtless David Cassidy was torn down from my bedroom wall) turned more serious when I spent all of my weekly allowances on thirty albums, stapled a hundred Elvis bubble-gum cards to the back of my bedroom door, and with white house paint and perfect Catholic-girl script wrote "Elvis" in three-foot letters all over my green bedroom walls. I remember his reading up on my prepubescent malady ("It's called 'hero worship,'" I heard him telling my mom) and his wondering aloud whether I needed a shrink.

Years later, when my tastes became more sophisticated and I dragged him along to see a Shakespeare play I was reviewing for my high school newspaper, he might have wished for the banality of a formulaic Elvis movie. "I can't understand a damn thing they're saying," he leaned over and whispered just as the second act was beginning.

Both of my true loves eluded him, but there was no time to talk about that now. In fact, there was hardly any talk at all. His speech was limited to whispers and hand motions; sometimes he would just point heavenward and then wave good-bye.

I never expected to be with Dad when he died.

I was the only one of his six grown daughters to live out of state. My five sisters, two younger half sisters, and adopted brother all lived near his home in Cincinnati. I was the one most likely to get the call after the fact. But I had visited Dad two weeks before, and he said something he had never said to me in any of my previous visits: "Please don't leave, Amy. I'll be sad." And then he balled up his hands and slowly raised them to his face. His hands swayed back and forth under his eyes, wiping away imaginary tears as a small child might. "I have to leave," I told him. Jeff and the kids were waiting for me at home. My plane was set to leave in a few hours.

The next morning he asked for me. Amy's gone back to Virginia, he was told. Later that day we talked by phone; he didn't remember why I had to go home. Was I still working on my Mister Rogers book? "No, I finished the manuscript two weeks ago," I said and tried to get off the phone before he could tell that I was crying. Dad had never taken account of my schedule before, but now he seemed to be looking for an opening. I had just gotten home, but I booked a flight back that day. This time the kids would come with me so I could stay for a few days longer. I called Dad back to let him know I would be there again in two weeks. "Wait for me," I told him.

I was standing near the back door of Dad's house, waiting to let his dog Buddy back in. My youngest sister, Tina, was leaning over Dad, who now spent all of his time in a hospital bed in his living room. "You seem sad, Dad," Tina said. "Are you okay?"

"I'm just missing Amy," he said. "I wish she would hurry up and get here." Tina looked up at me; I had already been there all afternoon.

Later I was sitting on his bed and feeding him the key lime pie his favorite Perkins waitress had brought by. (His other favorite waitress he had married, five years after he and my mom divorced. His wife, Patti, had died a year ago when her breast cancer spread, three months before he was diagnosed with lung cancer.) Tina was sitting on the other side of Dad. "When is Amy going to get here?" she asked in jest.

"Tomorrow at noon," Dad answered seriously as he took another bite from the fork I was holding.

"I don't think she's coming," Tina joked again. "I think she called to say she decided not to come because she's sick of your crap."

I rushed to my own defense: "That doesn't sound like Amy."

"No, it doesn't," Dad agreed. "It sounds like Tina." I laughed at Dad's unintentional comeback.

Tina insisted on keeping up the ruse: "No, it was Amy."

Dad never flinched: "Amy would never say that about her daddy."

Daddy.

He still referred to himself that way long after I had stopped. "Amy, this is your daddy," his answering machine messages would always begin. But he was right; I never would have said that. My loyalty to Dad wasn't always easy. He wasn't perfect, and his inability to show up for things—like my wedding—made it immeasurably more difficult to stick by him. My parents' divorce caused a permanent divide in the family, with the loyalties tipping in favor of my mom, who had chosen not to remarry. I don't know what made me stick by Dad. Maybe it was that he cared enough to think Elvis was causing me mental problems or that he sat through five acts of Shakespeare even though he didn't understand a thing they were saying.

Maybe it was my parochial school sensibilities. When my best friend, Patti Dattilo, asked me whether I was going to be part of the "new" generation of the seventies or part of the "old" generation of our parents—we were pulling up dandelions from the front yard of the convent that housed the nuns who taught at our elementary school (it was my idea)—I said "old." Things went better when you were obedient and loyal to those in authority over you, and if they were happy with the way things were, then I would be too. I was an old-school fourth grader, with fingers stained yellow by my good works.

———

At some point Dad realized I was there with him, that he wasn't still waiting on my arrival. But as eager as he had been for me to stay two weeks before, and as eager as I had been to see him again, my instinct was to keep my distance. I would naturally retreat to the kitchen after feeding him or giving him his medication. I sensed his deep need for privacy, as if something important was happening, something not to be interfered with.

I wouldn't have had the courage to respect that need three months earlier, when Dad was sent to a hospice center to die. It could be two hours or two weeks, the surgeon had told us, but this is definitely it. There was total panic among us siblings then, total selfishness. Possessiveness is a common reaction, the hospice nurse told me, when unfinished business must be resolved in hours instead of years. And it had been years for most of my sisters. Years of estrangement, years of excuses. Of course Dad had disappointed us. Of course he missed significant events in our lives. He was busy with his new family now. "Are you going to care who is right when he is in the grave?" I asked Tina when Dad had missed yet another of her daughter's birthday parties. We don't have a choice with parents. We honor them because we are supposed to. (It would have been just the thing I would have told Patti Dattilo while we were pulling dandelions out of the convent's front yard.)

So for many years it had been just Dad and me and eventually Tina (the "grave" question having won her over). But now the party was crowded with prodigals, all poring over our dying father, who was too sick to kill the fatted calf but celebrating nonetheless. And I was being crowded out, pushed to the edges of the room as they cried out in unison, "Daddy, please love me before you go."

I pushed back, attempting to reclaim my rightful place. But by then Dad had forgotten. The jubilant father, he was too busy covering over the dried pig slop with his best robes. "I have other daughters, you know," he said to me when I was lingering over a good-bye on my last day at the hospice center. His comment hurt, and what I wanted to say but didn't was, "Since when? Since they found out you were dying." I left the hospice center after a ten-day vigil to fly back home, hoping that wasn't the last thing my father ever said to me.

Three months later I was back. This was my third visit since we were told he had only two weeks to live. Dad never was good with expectations. This time I gave him his space. His quietness was so solemn I wondered if I should tiptoe in and out of the room where he stayed. Each time I gave him his medicine or tried to feed him, I felt as though I was interrupting something. As it turned out, I was.

Dad was making the decision—without pressure and without being doted over—to die.

I called the hospice nurse and told her my suspicions. She agreed that everyone should come to say their final good-byes.

Over the next few days, Dad was in and out. Most of the time he scanned the room with half-opened eyes, and then his whole body would jerk. When he tried to talk, it was a soft mumble. His eyes were still full of expression, but they expressed mostly frustration at our inability to understand him. He had no concept of time; he rambled on about World War II but never acknowledged the first anniversary of his wife's passing.

By Sunday afternoon I had already been there four days. My flight was set to leave the next day. I struggled with what to do. My kids' first day of school was two days away. What if Dad lingered for weeks? He had outsmarted death before, so much so that his hospice nurse Kelly had "Miracle Man" embroidered on a T-shirt for him. I called my husband. I talked to my oldest sister. She had called to talk to Dad, but he only made nonsense noises into the phone. "You'll know what to do when the time comes," she said just before I hung up the phone. I looked over at Dad. I realized that for the first time since I had arrived, I was completely alone with him in the house. My son and daughter were out walking Buddy; another sister, who had been spending the night, was at home for the time being. I smiled at him; he opened his mouth—and spoke. Clearly, even without his dentures. I wanted to call my sisters or run to get the kids, but I didn't dare leave his side should the Miracle Man go mute again. I held his hand. I told him my flight home was scheduled for the next day. "Is it okay if I go?" I asked.

His chin quivered. "No, it's not okay. Don't go. I'll be sad." It was the exact thing he had said to me during my last visit, and this time the tears were real. We kept talking. He picked up a photo of him and his nine children (the only one of all of us together), taken just after his wife's burial. "This was taken a year ago Saturday," he said matter-of-factly. He touched each person with his fingers as his eyes moved across the photo. I counted back the days in my head. He was right; Patti was buried the Saturday before Labor Day last year. *No one will ever believe me,* I thought. *Yesterday he was shooing World War II jet fighters, and today he is able to figure out to the day when his wife was buried.*

Still there were no interruptions. The phone didn't ring; the kids stayed outside with the dog. After a while, I decided to ask again. "Dad, I'm supposed to leave tomorrow. Is that okay?"

Tears returned to his soft brown eyes. "No," he said again. "Stay until it's over. I waited for you to come.

"You're going to be with me," he continued. "We're going to be alone. You're going to be holding my hand. It's going to get cold, icy cold, but you're going to be okay."

"Can I cry?" I asked.

"Yes, you can cry," he answered.

"Are you scared?"

"Not at all."

"But, Dad," I said, deeply moved but too logical to leave the obvious unsaid, "you have nine kids. There is no way we are going to be alone together when you die. It's not possible."

My half sister walked into the room and with a loud "Hey, Dad" shattered the oracle. Dad looked up at her, and when he opened his mouth, senseless mumbling tumbled out.

I went outside so he couldn't hear me crying, and as I did, my oldest sister pulled up in her car. "Is he dead?" she asked when she saw the state I was in. She had been away from Dad the longest, maybe fifteen years in all. She came back to take care of him as one of his primary caregivers when his cancer was diagnosed. I told her no, he wasn't dead, but he had just spoken to me, clearly. Without thinking, I told her what he had said. She didn't wait for me to finish but marched inside and went straight to Dad's bedside. "Do you want to be with Amy alone?" Her face was close to his.

"I want to be with Amy," he said, finding his voice again and producing for me a witness. "She's going to cry—a lot. But you know Amy; she'll be okay."

Dad's other primary caregiver while he had been sick was a sister who had been away from him nearly as long as the oldest. Coming back to care for him might have been their way of saying they were sorry, or maybe they were making up for lost time. As much as I appreciated their sacrifice, still it bothered me. When the prodigal son asked for his inheritance early, he was in essence saying to his father, "I wish you were dead." That's what estrangement says too. What I soon discovered, though, is that treating someone *as if he were dead* becomes more difficult when you find out he is dying. Intentions reverse when the person's existence is no longer determined by your saying so. It's the same reason breakups are more painful for the one being dumped; the power lies with the decision maker. Real death is permanent; pretend death is more flexible—you can reinvigorate the person at will. How careless we are with human life when we daydream.

Dad's usual bitterness and grumbling negativity dissolved when he found out he was dying, and to everyone's surprise, he was a pleasure to care for, deeply appreciative and loving. One of my sister-caregivers later said that she got to be with him during the best months of his life, without having to put up with his shortcomings (not the real word she used) on a day-to-day basis, as I had.

She felt fortunate.

But now there was even less of the appreciative and loving Dad to go around. As the days wore on, his gaze pulled to the left and stayed there, searching out things we couldn't see. To get any sort of acknowledgment, we had to sit on his left side and try to intercept his wandering eye. One of my estranged sisters claimed that chair. All the stray glances landed on her; all the random kisses touched her lips.

"Daddy, please love me before you go."

The "good son" began to stir within me.

But before I could rush in from the fields and disrupt the festivities, I caught a glimpse of the "Prayer of Saint Francis" framed and mounted on Dad's living room wall. Of all the beautiful sentiments in that poetic supplication, this one called to me the loudest: "Grant that I may not so much seek to be consoled as to console."

The gentle request became for me a stern warning. No more asking anything of Dad. I was there to console him, not to haggle over who deserved his final kisses.

So I did what I thought Dad would want: I dimmed the lights, shut off the TV for good, and played soft music, trying to model the birthing rooms where I had delivered my children. Death is similar to birth; they each have the same air of quiet expectation. We called it "the sanctuary."

People trickled in and out of Dad's sanctuary all week. Some understood the need for observance; others stumbled in and with their loud voices desecrated the place.

The sanctuary lacked one thing. I searched the house for a Bible. The only one I could find was old and discarded, with pages missing and no concordance. Dad had given me his Bible in December, nine months earlier, when he had first been diagnosed with cancer. "Aren't you going to need this?" I asked.

"No," he assured me; he had another one. "You take this one."

The Bible had been a gift from me, many years before. Someone at work had given him a Bible once, and it ended up in the trash can. He didn't throw mine out, but neither did he bother to crack its new binding (except to write, "Amy—Xmas '87," on the interior page). Dad despised "organized religion" and told horror stories of nuns the size of linebackers. One had called him stupid and made him repeat fourth grade, and he could never watch *The Sound of Music* after that. But when the church where his son attended day-care was making the evangelistic rounds one Saturday, with a list of day care parents' addresses, Dad gave them a chance. He was depressed, still in his bathrobe, and invited them in. They prayed for him, with him. ("They even made up their own prayers!" he told me afterward.) He pulled out the Bible I had given him two Christmases ago and had them sign it, as if they were rock stars or famous authors or simply people with the ability to change someone's life for eternity. And then he added his own note: "Amy's prayers answered—thank you. Tears of the Holy Spirit—the Lord spoke—the servant listened—March 4th, 1989. Gave my life to Jesus."

Now Dad was dying, and his Bible was back in Virginia. So I read his favorite psalms from the old Bible with pages missing.

———

It had been six days since Dad had eaten anything. I was sitting next to his bed (it didn't matter whether you were on his left or right; his eyes no longer searched), listening to Elvis and crying. I had bought one of Elvis's gospel albums during my "hero worship" phase, but I never felt quite right about looking to Elvis for religious inspiration. I passed the album off to Dad. He loved to listen to it in the dark, the lit end of his stogie slowly rising from the armrest to his mouth and back again.

He listened to the gospel album long after I left Elvis for others crushes (real boys, other celebrities, Freud). No one had remembered but me. I guess that's the problem with trying to make up for lost time when someone gets sick; you're not sure what was important to him when he was well. I played Elvis's rendition of "Peace in the Valley," and Dad moved ever so slightly.

Oh well, I'm tired and so weary, but I must go alone
Till the Lord comes and calls, calls me away, oh yes.[1]

On the same album was another hymn by Thomas A. Dorsey, written just after his wife had died giving birth. Elvis sang it with so much emotion, he sounded as if he was parodying himself.

Hold my hand, lest I fall
Take my hand, precious Lord, and lead me home.[2]

There were many tears and much hand-holding that night listening to Elvis. Then all the fluids drained out of Dad's body. It would only be a matter of hours now. I sat up all night in a straight-back chair with my arm propped up on the hospital bed railing. Every time Dad coughed or groaned, I squeezed his hand. He never squeezed back.

Dad was still there the next morning. The hospice nurse felt outwitted again; most people die within hours—at the most, twelve—once they release fluids. But Dad was still there, still refusing to meet expectations.

I was exhausted from having stayed up all night, trying to keep my promise to Dad. My sister Susan was ready to let me off the hook. "I don't think he meant it literally," she finally said. "He meant it figuratively. And you *have* held his hand through this whole transition, Amy. You sensed when he was making the decision to die. You read him his favorite psalms. You knew to turn off the TV and turn down the lights. You've done what he's asked you; you've held his hand. You're done."

Maybe she was right. The hospice workers had told us that the dying often choose their inner circle, those they want to be with when they die. Most of the time it's a person who has unfinished business with the dying person. And we all knew that wasn't me.

Dad made it through the day and night too. It was Saturday morning, September 11, and I had been there for ten days. Tina got up from her makeshift bed on the floor and fussed at Dad for taking so long. She called him a stubborn old man. She asked him what he was waiting for. ("That sounds like Tina," I could almost hear Dad saying.) She walked over to the jar she had filled with inspirational sayings and pulled one out, as she had every day since Dad began his descent. But today it was more of a rebuke than an inspiration: "Let us not go faster than God does," began the quote by Jacques Maritain.[3]

Tina got her answer; Dad was waiting for God. The sense of release was immediate. Everyone relaxed. We needed to be reminded that this was God's business. Katie took all the grand-kids to a movie. Beth went upstairs to take a nap. Susan was at her own home, showering. No more hovering or waiting on the stubborn old man.

Everyone had scattered, but I had no place to go. I was stay-ing at Dad's house, and since I was "on duty" when he started going downhill, I was in charge of his morphine, administered every two hours, day and night. I looked at my watch and told my sister Gigi, the only other person still in the room with me, that after I gave Dad his next dosage (he was due at 3:15), I was going to take a nap. I stretched out on the couch next to Dad's bed. I looked at my watch again, 3:13. Then I thought I heard the plas-tic sheet under Dad rustle, but that couldn't be right. He hadn't moved in days. (We later found out he had soiled himself.) I climbed up on his bed and took his hand. "This is Amy, Dad. Are you okay?" I told him the grandkids were at a movie, and Gigi and I were there in the room with him. He inhaled, but no breath came out. The hospice chaplain had told me that people can still hear for about two minutes after they stop breathing, so if we wanted to encourage Dad or tell him we loved him, he could still hear us. I expressed my encouragement (which came out awkwardly as "You did it, Dad!"), but as soon as he heard my voice, he released the stalled breath. Gigi began to panic and cry uncontrollably, and I motioned for her to go into the kitchen to gather herself. Dad's hand, limp for days, closed around mine and squeezed. He took another breath. It was exactly 3:15, but there would be no morphine and no nap. Dad was perfectly still. It was just the two of us—again—and I was holding his hand as he took his last breath, just as he had said.

Another ten-day vigil had come to a close; this one in death. The last one had ended with Dad's stinging words, "I have other daughters, you know." This one ended with the healing answer to a question I had been asking for nine months. If the prodigal son gets a party with a fatted calf and total absolution, I often wondered, what does the good son get? Dad had answered that for me: he gets to hold his father's hand while he takes his last breath.

We had unfinished business after all.

My Father's Gift

No one likes the good son in the prodigal son story (or Martha in the Mary and Martha story, for that matter). But the truth is, that's how I felt.

"The lostness of the resentful 'saint,'" Henri Nouwen wrote in *The Return of the Prodigal Son*, "is so hard to reach precisely because it is so closely wedded to the desire to be good and virtuous."[4]

Yes, that is true. I was the one with fingers stained yellow by my good works.

"The more I reflect on the elder son in me," Henri continued, "the more I realize how deeply rooted this form of lostness really is and how hard it is to return home from there. Returning home from a lustful escapade seems so much easier than returning home from a cold anger that has rooted itself in the deepest corners of my being."

I had cold anger and deep corners too; neither was deserving of a gift.

And yet I got one.

I held my father's hand as he took his last breath.

The hand-holding, being the only one with him when he died, wasn't the gift.

The gift was that he saw me in my deep corner as the homecoming party raged in the foreground. He saw me when I thought he had forgotten.

He cleared the room of partygoers and reached for my hand. Not to comfort himself as he died, but to dissolve my cold anger.

I wasn't being favored but healed.

Chapter 12

BACK TO THE WOODS

As a child, then, I had almost fallen into the well.
When grown up, I nearly fell into the word "eternity."

—NIKOS KAZANTZAKIS, *Zorba the Greek*

THIS QUOTE WAS given to me as a gift by Mr. Godar, my high school English teacher, when I was sixteen. Many years later (we kept in touch over the years through long letters), I would set before him Pascal's wager. Although I didn't know anything about Pascal or his wager at the time, I was just dangerous enough to make the flawed argument myself. I don't know if he read my letter or placed his bet. He was dying at the time. What I wanted for him above all was eternal life; what he wanted for me above all was that I spend my life writing. He must have known one day I would nearly fall into the word *eternity.*

But I did more than nearly fall. When I sat on the porch swing of the mountain cabin and longed to know the meaning of my father's dying gift, I didn't anticipate where that longing would take me. I didn't know that one day I would have my answer, but only after I had uncovered and deciphered the last gift the red thread had bound me to. It was not until I had written the last word of the last story that I was able to finish my own. The givers and receivers of dying gifts who fill the pages of this book became my teachers. I had to fall deeply into the well of their gifts before I could rightly divide my own.

My education, though, was not yet complete.

The Final Lesson

There is a maypole in my classroom.

That's what I'm thinking as I sit alone in the dark and listen to the ocean waves coming from my noise machine. It's really a "sound therapy relaxation system" with ten "soothing sounds," including thunder, a human heartbeat, and a waterfall. But almost always I listen to ocean waves.

I'm in the dark because I'm praying, and I focus better internally when I can't see. I don't pray out loud; in fact, I don't even think words in my head. Instead, I try to be perfectly silent. Silence is more important than words in prayer (one of the spiritual lessons Fred Rogers taught me).

Sometimes during these times of perfect quiet, images come to mind. I pay attention to them, because I am in silent prayer when they arrive.

On this particular evening, I see a classroom. I have seen this classroom once before, in my mind's eye, nearly two months ago (in the dark with ocean waves). It looks very much the same now as it did then. It is empty. There are desks but no students. There is a large pad of paper on an easel up front, to the left of the teacher's desk, if you're facing it. There is no chalk for the blackboards, but there is a big black marker at the base of the easel. The blank pages make me anxious. I don't like the marker; it can't be erased like chalk dust.

There is nothing esoteric in this image, I think to myself. If there is a message attached, it seems perfectly clear. I gave up my beloved college classroom to write full-time, traded a room crowded with challenging twenty-year-olds for the relative isolation of a writer's life. It is not the time for a crowded classroom. But there is a trade-off, evident in the image: marker is permanent, and chalk dust is not. Writing brings something into incontrovertible existence.

I write down the description of my classroom on a yellow legal pad and put it in between the pages of my Bible. There it sits for two months until I see the classroom in my mind's eye again.

This time I am busy writing on the easel up front. The only thing that has changed is that there is something new in the classroom. To the right of the teacher's desk and behind it is a wooden pole. It is not a flagpole (there is no flag and no place to hang or attach one if there was), and it is not a coat or hat rack (because there are no hooks). If you have only one hat or one coat, it might work.

For some reason the addition of the wooden pole seems important to me, so I sit a little longer in silence. Is there any significance to it? I feel nudged to try to figure it out myself (a nudge akin to the "silent shout" Gina heard in the attic). In my mind I try to imagine what it could be used for if I laid it sideways. It could be used to block the doorway, I suppose. Then I turn it upside down, but it can't stand that way because of the rounded top. I try to be creative, but it is just a wooden pole. I wait a few more minutes. Suddenly it occurs to me that if I slip a ring over the rounded top and pull ribbons through, my wooden pole could be used as a maypole.

There is a maypole in my classroom.

An interesting development, to be sure, but the only thing I know about maypoles is that they are danced around. Later I do a search online and find that the maypole is not simply the centerpiece of May Day festivities.

It is also a symbol of the *axis mundi*.

This is an interesting development, too, as an axis mundi (or world axis) is a thing or place that visibly or invisibly links heaven and earth. A concept found in architectural designs and religious imagery, an axis mundi not only serves as a connection between heaven and earth but can provide a pathway between the two, like Jacob's ladder: "a stairway resting on the earth, with its top reaching to heaven, and the angels of God . . . ascending and descending on it" (Gen. 28:12). Symbols range from this celestial stairway to church steeples that pierce the sky to trees that stretch their branches to the heavens (which is what the maypole stands for). There are sacred sites considered to be axes mundi, such as Calvary and the Mount of Olives. In ancient Mesopotamia, a temple-tower climbing skyward was given this unambiguous name: the House of the Link Between Heaven and Earth. I wonder if Henri's trapeze, his symbol of enfleshed spirituality, serves as a modern-day example. An axis mundi is a sacred space where—if only for a moment—heaven and earth are permitted to touch.

Now I know why there is a maypole in my classroom. It is there because in a singular image it captures the message of this book, one that I couldn't articulate without its arrival as I sat in the dark in silent prayer.

The dying themselves are an axis mundi, a connection, an intersection between heaven and earth. For a time, they bide between two worlds, providing for us a pathway. They lay tethered to eternity as we grasp onto them. What springs from this intersection, *what is left as proof of it*, is the gift of passage. It is why the red fern is said to live forever; it blossoms from these eternal seedlings. The sacred window passes; the gift remains.

Once when Jesus was teaching about gifts, he asked this question: "Which is greater: the gift, or the altar that makes the gift sacred?" (Matt. 23:19). Of course, it is what makes a gift sacred that is greater. Especially when the altar is heaven.

———

I am back at the same mountain cabin, on the same porch swing, where I sat a year ago, waiting for my dad to come out of the woods.

I think about what has happened since then, how I have been moved from story to story, from gift to gift—like the mythic hero on his journey—by an invisible hand, by the weavings of the red thread. Journey stories have common themes, and they often end the same way: in a reconciliation with the father. In most of these mythic odysseys, there is some paternal account that needs to be settled, a healing that can take place only by the father's hand.

A year has passed, and the red thread ties its knot for now. The last story has been unearthed, the last gift of passage unveiled. I am back at the same mountain cabin, but I am no longer looking for Dad. I have found him, I have found his healing, in the gift.

EPILOGUE

"YOU'RE THE ANGEL of death," my daughter says matter-of-factly as she licks around the edges of her melting ice cream cone.

It isn't a declaration I expect from my twelve-year-old at a coffee shop on a Saturday afternoon, but I recover enough to defend myself. "The angel of death *brings* death, honey. I'm not the angel of death. I don't cause people to die."

Steadied by another sip of coffee (and thankful no one is close enough to overhear the exchange), I add, "I just end up talking to people about their grief—a lot."

My kids were used to it by now. Emily had just finished her first softball practice, and, of course, I found the one mother there who was grieving and engaged her in conversation for the length of the practice. The mother felt fortunate that I was willing to talk to her about her loss; the mother sitting between us did not.

She listened patiently for a while, then got up to look through the fence and offer her daughter some tips. When she returned, she used the opportunity to scoot her folding chair back a little, discreetly excusing herself from all the death talk. No reason to spoil a spring afternoon unless you have to.

I understand her disengagement. The conversation wasn't relevant to her. When I once gave a friend a copy of *Streams in the Desert*, a book I'd found solace in for years, she confessed, "It's too depressing. I try to read it, but it's all negative." Later, when she was going through a particularly rough time, she pulled it down from the bookshelf. It became healing water to her, a stream in the desert.

God's "choicest cordials [are] kept for our deepest faintings," Lottie Cowman wrote in the foreword to *Streams in the Desert*.[1] That's why my friend initially found the book too negative; it's why the woman next to me at softball practice scooted back. Neither was fainting.

But when you are, as the other woman at softball practice was—her husband had died of a massive heart attack and she was raising their five children alone—you find it hard to talk about anything else.

Especially if the "angel of death" is two chairs down.

———

Things would be easier on my kids now that the book was written, now that I understood Dad's dying gift to me. I would be less likely to embarrass them with my death talk.

The journey was over, my task completed. I had descended to the netherworld and returned with a boon. Life was tidy again.

A few short weeks passed in which I talked to strangers only about the weather. Then the letter arrived.

It was from Bertha's daughter-in-law. I hadn't talked to Bertha, my unlikely eighty-six-year-old friend, since Christmas, but I had dreamed about her a few days before. *The dream was a shadow from the book,* I thought upon waking, left over, since in the dream Bertha had died.

In the dream Bertha had died, and no one had remembered to invite me to the funeral. The "angel of death" left off the guest list.

I met Bertha ten years ago, but we hadn't lived in the same town for many years now. I usually talked to her at Christmas (when we first met) and on her birthday. Bertha lived alone, and once, years ago, I became concerned when I called and she didn't answer the phone or return my call. Instead, I got a note in the mail: "I'm not dead, if that's what you're wondering," she had written.

That's what I was wondering, then and now.

———

Bertha was housebound, bedridden, and vodka soaked when I first met her. We had recently moved to her small town (the same town Junior lived in), and we were still getting to know our neighbors. I must have been feeling the holiday spirit, because on a busy Christmas Eve I decided to venture over to Bertha's house. I had invited her adult son, who lived with her at the time, to our home on Christmas Day and wondered if his mother would like to come too. "She doesn't leave the house," he told me, "but you can go in and ask her."

I walked into Bertha's dim bedroom. "It's about time," she

growled, her expectation that the new preacher's wife in town should have made the shut-in rounds long before now. "You're awful pretty, aren't you?" she asked, more an accusation than a compliment. "Get where I can see you."

Maybe I found the only soft spot left in Bertha, and maybe she unearthed some hidden pluck in me. It's not always easy to explain why people become friends. But long after we moved away and closer ties to the town were left untended, Bertha and I stayed connected.

We were no longer neighbors when I visited her in the hospital after heavy drinking caused her to fall and seriously injure herself.

Or when I visited her at her home after she dried out and gave up her bed for a wheelchair.

Or when I calmly explained to her as she yelled at me on the phone for not sending her a Christmas card that it was because my dad had just died and I didn't feel like being festive. "It's been two years with no card," she reminded me harshly. ("That's because I didn't feel like being festive when he was first diagnosed with cancer either," I threw back.) In her mind two years was plenty of time for life to become tidy again.

Then the letter from her daughter-in-law arrived.

———

Bertha was not dead. But she had fallen again (this time due to old age) and been hospitalized. While in the hospital, she suffered a stroke. She now lay blind and half paralyzed in a nursing home.

"How did she know to write you?" Bertha asked when I made the trip down south that weekend to see her.

"I guess she found my letters as she was going through your things," I said. A few dozen letters and cards and a gold angel pin, evidence of our friendship.

"I'm blind as a bat, you know," she said.

No more "pretty" insults; no more "Get where I can see you."

"I had a dream about you," I said, leaving out the details. "And then a few days later Marion's letter arrived."

"You have good instincts," she said.

Or maybe I had learned the lesson I was meant to. The lesson that the angel of death—the real angel of death—isn't to be feared as a taker only. He also leaves gifts.

I knew to expect it now.

NOTES

CHAPTER 1

1. C. S. Lewis, *A Grief Observed* (New York: Bantam Books, 1961), 148.
2. Wilson Rawls, *Where the Red Fern Grows* (New York: Bantam Books, 1974), 247.

CHAPTER 2

1. Mark Moring, "The Man Behind the Wardrobe," *Christianity Today*, October 31, 2005, http://www.christianitytoday.com/movies/interviews/douglashgresham.html.
2. Garrison Keillor, "Let's Not Be Beastly to a Harvard Man," *Free Lance-Star* (Fredericksburg, VA), July 30, 2005.
3. Lewis, *A Grief Observed*, 4.
4. C. S. Lewis, *The Four Loves* (San Diego: Harcourt Brace Jovanovich, 1960), 131.
5. Chad Walsh, afterword to C. S. Lewis, *A Grief Observed*, 151.
6. Technically, the main character is a half sister, not a stepsister, an element I've tweaked here because the ugly stepsister is a more common fairy-tale invention than the ugly half sister.
7. C. S. Lewis, *Till We Have Faces: A Myth Retold* (San Diego: Harcourt, 1956), 292.
8. Lewis, *A Grief Observed*, 30–31.
9. Joan Didion, *The Year of Magical Thinking* (New York: Alfred A. Knopf, 2005), 44.
10. Walter Hooper, *C. S. Lewis: A Companion and Guide* (San Francisco: HarperSanFrancisco, 1996), 250.
11. Lewis, *A Grief Observed*, 53–54.

CHAPTER 3

1. MercyMe, *Almost There*, DVD, interview excerpt and song lyrics (New York: Sony BGM Music Entertainment, 2005).
2. Blaise Pascal, *Pensées* (London: Penguin Classics, 1995), 127.
3. Blaise Pascal, quoted in John R. Tyson, *Invitation to Christian*

Spirituality: An Ecumenical Anthology (New York: Oxford University Press, 1999), 293–94.

CHAPTER 4

1. Meister Eckhart, *Meister Eckhart: A Modern Translation* (New York: Harper & Row, 1941), 243.
2. Gaston Leroux, *The Phantom of the Opera* (Englewood Cliffs, NJ: Globe Book Company, 1993), 1.
3. Carrie Hernandez, "Part III: The Origin of the Legend (Interview with Sandra Andrés Belenguer)," http://www.phantomoftheopera.info/sandra03.htm.
4. Quotes in this section are from Leroux, *Phantom of the Opera*, 99, 170, 15, respectively.
5. Charles Hart and Richard Stilgoe (lyrics), Andrew Lloyd Webber (music), *The Phantom of the Opera* (London: Really Useful Group, 1986).
6. Ibid.
7. Quotes in this section are from Leroux, *Phantom of the Opera*, 177, 178, respectively.
8. Cathy Dyson, "A Bright Spot in a Week of Mourning," *Free Lance-Star* (Fredericksburg, VA), March 1, 2006.
9. Leroux, *Phantom of the Opera*, 184.

CHAPTER 5

1. Saint Thérèse de Lisieux, Catholic Online, http://www.catholic.org/saints/saint.php?saint_id=105.
2. Quotes in this section are from Mary Ann Sullivan, "What Mother Teresa Is Still Teaching Us," *Catholic Twin Circle*, January 1998.
3. Maggie Callanan and Patricia Kelley, *Final Gifts: Understanding the Special Awareness, Needs, and Communications of the Dying* (New York: Poseidon Press, 1992), 179.

CHAPTER 6

1. He typed it exactly as I wrote it, and I was embarrassed by the fact that I had used "saddening," which a teacher later informed me was not a word. I recently discovered that she was wrong; it is a word, used both as a verb and as an adjective. I have better instincts with language than with epidermal layers.
2. Frederick Buechner, *A Room Called Remember: Uncollected Pieces* (San Francisco: Harper & Row, 1984), 152–53.
3. Pamela Ribon, *Why Girls Are Weird* (New York: Pocket Books, 2003), 296.

4. Fred Rogers, in a radio interview with *Decision Today*, Billy Graham Evangelistic Association, August 7, 2002.

5. Frederick Buechner, *Whistling in the Dark: An ABC Theologized* (San Francisco: Harper & Row, 1988), 100.

6. Ibid.

7. Amy Hollingsworth, *The Simple Faith of Mister Rogers: Spiritual Insights from the World's Most Beloved Neighbor* (Nashville: Thomas Nelson, 2005), 80.

8. Fred Rogers, quoted in Wendy Murray Zoba, "Won't You Be My Neighbor?" *Christianity Today*, March 2000.

9. Peter Kreeft, "What Will Heaven Be Like?" *Christianity Today*, June 2003.

10. Sam Hawken, whose writings can be found at www.samhawken.com.

11. C. S. Lewis, *The Silver Chair* (New York: HarperTrophy, 1994), 252.

12. Kreeft, "What Will Heaven Be Like?"

CHAPTER 7

1. Connie Kiernan, *Signs of Approaching Death* (1997).

2. Ethelbert Stauffer, quoted in George R. Beasley-Murray, *John*, Word Biblical Commentary (Waco, TX: Word Books, 1987), 349.

3. Charles Dickens, *The Adventures of Oliver Twist* (New York: Illustrated Editions Company), 287.

4. Ralph W. Klein, *1 Samuel*, Word Biblical Commentary (Waco, TX: Word Books, 1983), 176.

5. Roswell D. Hitchcock, *An Interpreting Dictionary of Scripture Proper Names*, http://www.biblestudytools.net/Dictionaries/HitckcocksBibleNames/hbn.cgi?number=T933, s.v. "Goliath."

6. F. B. Meyer, quoted in *Streams in the Desert*, ed. Mrs. Charles E. Cowman, (Los Angeles: Oriental Missionary Society, 1931), 289.

CHAPTER 8

1. Jean Fritz, *The Great Little Madison* (New York: Putnam, 1989), 150.

2. A. Hayward, *Autobiography, Letters, and Literary Remains of Mrs. Piozzi (Thrale)* (Boston: Ticknor & Fields, 1861), introduction.

3. Henri Nouwen, *Sabbatical Journey: The Diary of His Final Year* (New York: Crossroad Classics, 1998), back cover.

4. George Leybourne, "The Man on the Flying Trapeze," lyrics and music (New York: C. H. Ditson & Co., 1868).

5. Henri Nouwen, *Our Greatest Gift: A Meditation on Dying and Caring* (San Francisco: HarperSanFrancisco, 1994), 66.

6. Nouwen, *Sabbatical Journey*, 194–95 (emphasis added).

7. This quote and the two that follow are from Nouwen, *Our Greatest Gift*, 67.

8. This quote and the two that follow are from William Saroyan, *The Daring Young Man on the Flying Trapeze: And Other Stories* (New York: New Directions Publishing Corporation, 1997), 19–26.

9. Emily Dickinson, "Death Sets a Thing Significant," *The Complete Poems of Emily Dickinson* (Boston: Little, Brown, 1924), 53.

10. Mary Ann Lickteig, "Cartoonist Charles Schulz Dies at 77," Salon.com, February 13, 2000, http://archive.salon.com/people/obit/2000/02/13/schulz/index.html.

11. Nouwen, *Sabbatical Journey*, 4.

12. Michael Zitz, "Stafford Sports Icon Dies," *Free Lance-Star* (Fredericksburg, VA), November 21, 2006.

13. This quote and the two that follow are from Nouwen, *Sabbatical Journey*, 168, 87, 122, respectively.

14. Ibid.

CHAPTER 9

1. Clifton Fadiman and André Bernard, *Bartlett's Book of Anecdotes* (Boston: Little, Brown, 2000), 4.

2. According to Thomas Wentworth Higginson's letter of August 16, 1870; letter later published in *Atlantic Monthly*, October 1891.

3. Emily Dickinson, *The Letters of Emily Dickinson*, vol. 2, ed. Thomas H. Johnson (Cambridge: Belknap Press of Harvard University Press, 1958), 570.

4. Thomas Wentworth Higginson, quoted in Margaret H. Freeman, "Emily Dickinson," *The Literary Encyclopedia*, January 11, 2005, http://www.litencyc.com/php/speople.php?rec=true&UID=1259.

5. C. S. Lewis, *A Grief Observed* (New York: Bantam Books, 1961), 68–69.

6. Maggie Callanan and Patricia Kelley, *Final Gifts: Understanding the Special Awareness, Needs, and Communications of the Dying* (New York: Poseidon Press, 1992), 113–116.

7. Cathy Dyson, "Man Left Priceless Message," *Free Lance-Star* (Fredericksburg, VA), December 30, 2005.

8. Kimberly Osias and Brian Todd, "Miner's Final Note," CNN.com, January 6, 2006, http://www.cnn.com/2006/US/01/06/miner.note/.

9. Emily Dickinson, "I've Seen a Dying Eye," in *The Complete Poems of Emily Dickinson* (Boston: Little, Brown, 1924), 15.

CHAPTER 10

1. Thomas Merton, *The Seven Storey Mountain* (San Diego: Harcourt Brace, 1998), 462.

2. Quotes by Thomas Merton in this chapter are from Thomas Merton, *The Intimate Merton: His Life from His Journals* (San Francisco: HarperSanFrancisco, 1999), 72, 158, 246, 284, 246, respectively.
3. James S. Torrens, "'Original Child Bombs' and Other Gems," review of *In the Dark Before Dawn*, edited by Lynn R. Szabo, *America*, May 9, 2005.
4. This quote and the two that follow are from Hermann Hesse, *Steppenwolf* (New York: Picador USA, 2002), 15–17.
5. Lisa Dahm, "Author Relishes Chance to Introduce 'New' Poetry by Merton," *Catholic News Service* (Honolulu, HI), October 2005.

CHAPTER 11

1. Thomas A. Dorsey, "Peace in the Valley," lyrics and music (New York: Unichappell Music Inc., 1939, renewed 1951).
2. Thomas A. Dorsey, "Take My Hand, Precious Lord," lyrics and music (New York: Unichappell Music Inc., 1938, renewed 1965).
3. Quoted in Jean-luc Barre and Bernard Doering, trans., *Jacques and Raissa Maritain: Beggars for Heaven* (Notre Dame, IN: University of Notre Dame Press, 2005), 94.
4. This quote and the one that follows are from Henri Nouwen, *The Return of the Prodigal Son: A Story of Homecoming* (New York: Doubleday, 1994), 69, 75, respectively.

EPILOGUE

1. L. B. Cowman, *Streams in the Desert* (Los Angeles: Oriental Missionary Society, 1925), foreword.